√15

FIRST TO JUMP

FIRST TO JUMP

HOW THE BAND OF BROTHERS WAS AIDED BY THE
BRAVE PARATROOPERS OF PATHFINDERS COMPANY

Jerome Preisler

BERKLEY CALIBER, NEW YORK

THE BERKLEY PUBLISHING GROUP
Published by the Penguin Group
Penguin Group (USA) LLC
375 Hudson Street, New York, New York 10014

USA • Canada • UK • Ireland • Australia • New Zealand • India • South Africa • China

penguin.com

A Penguin Random House Company

This book is an original publication of The Berkley Publishing Group.

Library of Congress Cataloging-in-Publication Data

Preisler, Jerome.
First to jump : how the band of brothers was aided by the brave paratroopers
of pathfinders company / Jerome Preisler. — First edition.
pages cm
ISBN 978-0-425-26597-0
1. United States. Army—Parachute troops—History—World
War, 1939–1945. 2. World War, 1939–1945—Campaigns—Western Front.
3. Parachute troops—United States—History—20th century. I. Title.
D769.347.P74 2014
940.54'1273—dc23
2014029242

First edition: December 2014

PRINTED IN THE UNITED STATES OF AMERICA

10 9 8 7 6 5 4 3 2 1

Interior text design by Tiffany Estreicher

In memory of Elmer and Noni Kosinski,
who bridged the damages of war with their love.

They were considered mavericks, insubordinates, and undesirables, and they'd done plenty to earn the reputation. Their commanding officers were glad, not to say overjoyed, to see them ship out to train for their special missions—glad just to be rid of them, never mind that those missions were thought to be suicidal.

They were the U.S. Army Pathfinders of the IX Troop Carrier Command. The first paratroopers to jump into combat.

And they were heroes to a man.

I spent two years chronicling their story to fill a significant gap in the history of the U.S. airborne military effort during World War Two—and in the much broader history of special operations commandos in the U.S. armed services.

While there is some excellent literature about the 101st "Screaming Eagles" and 82nd Airborne Divisions, not much has been said of their Pathfinder units, perhaps because a lot of information about their covert actions, tactics, and equipment remained classified for decades after the war, and also possibly because they were relatively small in number—fewer than three hundred of them jumped into Normandy in June 1944, and only about two dozen into the frigid, snow-blanketed heart of Bastogne later that year, on the third and arguably most daring mission for which their unique expertise was required. If not for the Pathfinders' heroic pinpoint drop into a German siege ring consisting of a quarter million infantry troops and more than a thousand tanks, the Christmas airlift of vital supplies and ammunition to the city's encircled U.S. forces might have failed or never gotten underway. Without it Bastogne would have been lost, the cost in American lives would have soared, and the Allied cause would have been severely damaged—or worse.

The Pathfinders were by definition special advance teams. Their job, put succinctly, was to jump behind enemy lines and mark the drop zones and landing zones for the main waves of airborne troops to follow. This alone made their existence a military innovation. But as conceived and refined by Acting Lieutenant Colonel Joel L. Crouch and Acting Sergeant Jake McNiece, the Pathfinders' jump into Bastogne helped lay the blueprint for the sort of surgical strikes that would gain subsequent elite units widespread—and well-deserved—public recognition.

My intent here isn't to subtract from the accomplishments of any of those other groups. Rather, it's to enrich the story of their conceptual and tactical development and give the Pathfinders their full due as trailblazers in every sense of the word.

The brainchild of Lieutenant Crouch and the 82nd Airborne's General James M. Gavin, the Pathfinders were created as a result of—and antidote to—the confusion that beset Gavin's airborne jump into Sicily during the 1943 Allied invasion of the island. As his 505th Parachute Regiment troops had flown there across the Mediterranean, German flak, friendly fire, and windblown combat smoke forced many of his paratroopers to evacuate their beleaguered C-47 transport planes and become scattered behind enemy lines.

Hiking toward the beachhead with only his compass and the sounds of battle to guide him, Gavin had assembled stray groups of wounded and disoriented paratroopers into a ragtag fighting band. Before all was said and done, his parachute infantrymen would become involved in several important—and bloody—clashes with the enemy. But as a result of their chaotic drop, they sustained terrible losses and accomplished few of their intended objectives.

After Sicily, Gavin consulted with several American and British Air Force generals about how to avoid similar disasters in the future. He then turned to Lieutenant Crouch, a pioneer in civilian air transport and ace troop carrier pilot, to develop the tactics and training methods for commando-style teams that would jump ahead of the main waves of paratroopers without support, stealing across enemy terrain to scout and mark out drop zones with an array of top secret homing and guidance equipment.

In early 1944, Crouch established the Pathfinder School at RAF North Witham in Lincolnshire, England. Sheer nerve and soldiering ability were absolute requirements for a trooper to make the final grade. But so dangerous were the planned missions—there was an anticipated fatality rate of 80 or 90 percent—that most of the men enticed to take the all-volunteer training were considered troublemakers by their COs and had been persuaded it was a way to rehabilitate their tarnished service records or even avoid the brig. It is arguable, however, that the same maverick qualities that made them what Jake McNiece called bad "garrison" soldiers gave them the adaptivity needed to survive and carry out their goals under conditions their training had only approximated. The book on Pathfinding was in a real sense written on the fly by troopers whose psychological and emotional wiring freed them to toss out the rules and improvise when circumstances demanded it.

But the men who jumped only account for part of this story. The rest is about the brave and innovative aircrews who flew them to their destinations.

Along with the paratroopers, top-notch pilots and crews from each of the army's troop carrier groups were sent to North Witham for rigorous retraining under Crouch, who would teach them stealthy air delivery techniques for the advance paratrooper teams—and rapid getaway methods through enemy flak once they'd dropped their troop loads. Meanwhile, the Pathfinders would undergo endless drills in the British countryside, where they practiced using their Eureka radar transmitters, fluorescent signal panels, and colored smoke for their first mission.

That mission would be no less critical to Allied fortunes than Operation Overlord—the D-Day invasion of Normandy. And it is with D-Day—or the night before, when the Pathfinders left England a short while ahead of the rest of the airborne troops—that this tale begins.

As a note, I've primarily focused here on the Pathfinders of the 101st Airborne Division, but in no way do I mean to ignore or minimize the actions of the 82nd Airborne Division Pathfinders who courageously jumped in the same campaigns. My decision was based almost altogether on practical considerations; in order to tell the tale most clearly, a narrative line had to be drawn, and staying with the 101st seemed the best and straightest course.

It is my honor and privilege to share with you the exploits of the Pathfinders and the airmen who risked everything to fly them into combat. I am profoundly humbled by their courage and will be ever grateful for their sacrifices.

—JEROME PREISLER
JULY 2014

NORMANDY

JUNE 5–7, 1944

When you land in Normandy, you will have only one
friend: God.

—General James Gavin
to the Pathfinders on D-Day Minus One

CHAPTER ONE

1.

Captain Frank Lillyman, 502nd Parachute Infantry Regiment, 101st Airborne Division, knew his Pathfinders would have moonlight in their favor—a full moon and his lucky cigar. It had been clenched between his front teeth during each of his previous forty-seven jumps and was poking out of his mouth now for jump forty-eight, his first into combat. He called it a pet superstition and had only gotten burned on a single occasion.

Whenever Lillyman ran low on stogies—the Army rationed twelve a week—he would write his curly-haired missus back in Skaneateles, New York, and ask her to send spares all the way from home. He wrote Jane a lot of letters, and kept her as informed about what he was doing with the paratroopers as the military censors would allow.

At the airdrome several hours before takeoff, he and another paratroop officer had hammed it up with their veteran pilot, Lieutenant Colonel Joel Crouch, for the filming of an official War Department newsreel.

Crouch sported jump wings on his lapel, and the airborne officers had good-naturedly teased him about it. These wings were worn with pride when paratroopers graduated jump training school. They normally didn't like anyone outside their select brotherhood putting them on, but Crouch was an exception.

A top United Airlines pilot in civilian life, the colonel had made nine practice jumps to get a better grasp of what paratroopers experienced in action. After the nearly disastrous airborne attack on Sicily in 1943, he'd brainstormed the idea of Pathfinder sticks with General "Jumping" James Gavin, one of the fathers of the U.S. parachute infantry. Crouch was the definition of an ace, and no flier in the armed forces had garnered more respect among the sky soldiers.

Tonight he and his aircrew were flying the lead plane of the D-Day invasion into the teeth of the enemy's defenses, carrying the Pathfinders behind German lines. Once on the ground, the jumpers would be on their own, operating without support to mark the drop zones for the main airborne invasion waves. Crouch had pinned the badge on his uniform to honor their courage, and when the paratroopers had seen it there, worn close to his heart, they'd understood and appreciated the gesture.

In the weeks they'd spent awaiting their mission orders, the Pathfinders had found ample time to ponder their odds of surviving the mission. None had entertained any illusion, and how could they?

Their own leaders, including Gavin himself, had told them those odds were slim to none.

2.

On the morning of June 5, 1944, General Dwight D. Eisenhower, Supreme Commander of the Allied Expeditionary Force, had been faced with a crucial decision. After days of stormy weather, there was no assurance the clouds would break long enough to launch the invasion.

The window for Operation Overlord was narrow. It would either start between June 4 and 7 or be postponed at least two weeks, until the tide off Normandy would again be low around sunrise. That was essential if the mine-clearing teams were to wade into the shallows and do their job, enabling the aquatic landing craft to approach the beachhead.

Eisenhower knew any delay would be less than ideal for the paratroopers. In two weeks the nights that preceded an early morning low tide would be moonless. The Pathfinders, and the main wave of thirteen thousand sky troopers whose way they would light, would have to jump behind enemy lines in pitch-darkness.

Now they were ready to go—and getting nervous. They had been waiting near the airfield for more than thirty-six hours, and their restless expectancy had originated long before. By late May, the men had known the invasion was in the offing, although its commencement date had been kept top secret. That had been preceded by months of training at RAF North Witham, not far from Nottinghamshire, where Robin Hood and his band had been legendary thorns in the sheriff's side. While out on their weekend passes, the paratroopers would carry on their own rowdy exploits at village pubs, sometimes getting into trouble with the latter-day constabulary, and leaving Lillyman to sweet-talk them out of it.

Once in their marshaling areas, the Pathfinders had quartered in makeshift tent cities behind barbed wire fencing, guarded by machine gun–toting military police from another division. It was hardly an ideal situation. In fact, it made them feel more like prisoners than they ever had in Nottingham's revolving-door guardhouse. As one paratrooper would write, "The only comparable sensation would be those last five days in the death house, when everybody is quiet and considerate and they feed you well and let you sleep late and write letters and give you little favors and comforts."

Conversation with the MPs was forbidden, and only the officers were allowed in or out of the marshaling area. The troopers attended countless briefings that made use of elaborate sand table replicas of the Normandy countryside, allowing them to study miniature re-creations of roads, streams, canals, farms, hedgerows, and German military emplacements near the drop zones. Their knowledge of the invasion plan was the reason for the high security. Allied leaders were concerned about German spies and infiltrators, and did not want to risk the paratroopers talking to outsiders about the D-Day preparations.

The troopers had responded well to these restrictions. To pass the time, they'd written letters, played volleyball, sparred in organized boxing matches, and amused themselves with endless rounds of blackjack and craps. Inspired by a 1939 movie about the fearsome Apache warrior Geronimo, Army parachutists had taken to shouting his name as a battle cry when they jumped out of planes. While awaiting their invasion orders, they'd given each other haircuts that they named after the Indian chief, shaving the sides of their heads bare and leaving a long strip of hair in the middle.

Still, General Eisenhower had known the men could only keep their feelings of restlessness and isolation at bay for so long, and had wrestled with the state of their morale in contemplating later dates. Bowed with the weight of his responsibility, he would pace about his command tent at Southwick, and had often shrugged into his trench coat and taken long, solitary walks in the rain and dampness. How would more weeks of anxious anticipation affect them? And what of the sailors and infantry aboard the vessels at sea? The lives of two million men hung on his decision. "The mighty host was tense as a coiled spring," Eisenhower later penned. Surely it would wear on their psyches and be even harder if their commanders waited a full month for optimal lunar and tidal conditions.

SCAEF Eisenhower had consulted with his meteorologists twice a day, polling his coalition leaders for their opinions. Finally he'd decided. He would move forward with the operation, hoping the predictions of a letup in the rainy weather held true.

Toward the evening of June 5, the hundred and twenty Pathfinders were brought a mile north of the marshaling area to the airfield, where they assembled into groups called jump sticks. Each stick was joined by riflemen from the 508th Parachute Infantry Regiment who had been assigned to provide cover while they set out their equipment.

Besides the seventy-pound combat loads of weapons, rations, medical supplies, and other assorted gear carried by jumpers in all airborne units, the Pathfinders bore with them secret equipment that would be used to guide the main waves of paratroopers toward their drop zones: Eureka radar sets, Holophane light panels, and colored smoke grenades to be used for daylight landings, when the panels couldn't be seen from above. The men had nicknamed this special array the "ol' scarf," after the neckerchiefs that Hollywood Western heroes would hang from trees and bushes to mark their trailheads—in other words, mark their paths—so that others could follow when they went riding off after the cowboys with the black hats.

A stick of paratroopers was typically composed of eight men, but the experimental Pathfinder teams had from ten to twelve jumpers. This was because their casualty rate was projected at about 80 percent. The brass expected six out of eight Pathfinders to be killed in action, so they gave them extra manpower. Moreover, each radar and light operator had a specific role in laying out the DZ, and a backup on the team who could perform it if he was killed or wounded. Building redundancy, atop redundancy, to each drop zone, the military would assign two Pathfinder sticks with the same mission and equipment. If the entire primary stick was incapacitated before it could finish its task, the secondary group would be ready take its place.

Being the first to jump into hostile territory was extremely risky business, and the men who were accepted for Pathfinder training had to be the toughest of the tough. A paratrooper qual was of course a requirement. Word had gone out for soldiers with radio communications experience, especially those skilled at Morse code. But it was difficult to find volunteers for what many considered the definition of a suicide mission. For that reason a fair number of them were noncommissioned officers who'd gotten in hot water because of their difficulties with conventional soldiering— disciplinary problems, in other words. The incentive for becoming a Pathfinder, then, was often that it presented those men with an alternative to military punishment . . . or, looking at it another way, with a chance to buff up their service records and rehabilitate their standing within the ranks.

The Pathfinders attached to the 502nd PIR of the 101st Airborne—the Screaming Eagles—would be transported across the English Channel in twenty Dakota Skytrains. Adapted from the civilian DC-3 airliners Lieutenant Crouch had flown in what seemed another lifetime, the large, sturdy twin props had black and white invasion stripes painted near their tails to make them identifiable to Allied antiaircraft batteries. Friendly fire had been one of the major problems with the paratrooper drop on Sicily, causing terrible loss and confusion as offshore guns opened up on arriving flights, and the goal was to avoid a repeat of that debacle this time. But Crouch and the rest of the airmen who would fly the Pathfinders to their destination knew they'd have to make it past the formidable German shore defenses, itself a daunting proposition.

This coordinated airborne assault was to begin right around midnight.

Going in first without backup, the Pathfinders would jump into enemy territory a half hour earlier.

3.

The first to leave the runway, Lieutenant Crouch's plane—tail number 23098—soared into the night sky at 9:54 P.M., with the rest taking wing at five-minute intervals. Once they reached cruising altitude, they assembled into tight V formations: three planes to a V serial, three V serials to an echelon.

The pilots were taking their cue from nature. Like geese during long migrations, flying in these groups allowed them to maintain closer contact and communication in the air.

Whipcord thin at 140 pounds—although he weighed twice that in full uniform and gear—Captain Lillyman sat behind the cockpit chewing his customary cigar. The men always kept an eye out for it, reasoning that the luck it brought him could only be an asset for them too. In fact, during a practice jump over England with his Pathfinder trainees, he'd neglected to put the stogie in his mouth and their whole mood had changed. Glancing at their faces as they neared the target, he'd decided something was wrong.

"Hey," he asked one of them, "what's the trouble with you fellas?"

"The captain hasn't got his cigar," the trooper replied.

With that, Lillyman had taken one out of his pocket and chomped down on it so all the men could see. As he recalled, the plane had made an additional circle of the field, and the stick had jumped with their usual swagger . . . *and* a full measure of good luck, they would have agreed.

Of course Lillyman's confidence stemmed from much more than just the lucky cigar. He knew his men inside out. Most weren't big on rules and would have admitted to having had a close brush or two—or possibly three—with insubordination. But, then again, he'd heard whispers that his own regimental commander, Colonel George van Horn Moseley, had called him an "arrogant smart-ass" behind his back before he'd gotten assigned to head up the Pathfinder training school.

If this was true, he was okay with it. He was proud of his unit. In his opinion, a maverick disposition was almost an essential quality for its fighters. It went along with a strong sense of independence and was partly what would allow them to seize the initiative and make quick decisions under pressure. In short, it gave them the wherewithal to do their job knowing they would sink or swim on their own.

Looking down the aisle at his troopers, Lillyman could have given a detailed recitation of their temperaments, backgrounds, and specialized skills. For instance, Private Gus Mangoni, the demolition man, was the best he'd ever seen at working with a stick of dynamite. Along with John "The Greek" Zamanakos, Mangoni could do just about anything he wanted setting an explosion. They were quite a team.

Private John McFarlen was in position to be the third to jump behind Lillyman. An ornery, rough-and-tumble Texan, he enjoyed fighting for the simple fun of it and had prompted many an aggravated Saturday night phone call to the Nottingham police after a fracas at the local pub. McFarlen was one of the guys for whom a three-day pass usually spelled *trouble*, and Lillyman had had his hands full keeping him out of the English guardhouse. But now McFarlen was hot to go up against the German Army, and that was their great misfortune.

Private Frank Rocca—the boys called him "The Rock"—was cut from the same toughened mold, a born scrapper. Knee-high to a keg of cider and hard as a barrel of nails, he knew how to handle an M-1 carbine as well as anyone. On the firing range, he'd show off his skill by weaving like a hula dancer with the Tommy gun at his hip as he turned silhouette targets to splinters.

The unit's scouts, Privates Frederik Wilhelm and Bluford Williams, sat toward the rear of the troop section, and Lillyman would have followed them anywhere without hesitation. Williams was also his cleanup man, the last Pathfinder in line aboard the plane. His orders were to keep pushing the stick forward in case anybody got cold feet . . . though Williams had mused to himself that the door was so tight, it would have been hard to budge a man in full jump gear out of it.

Seated between Williams and the security detachment, saying little and keeping to themselves, were a Section 2 intelligence liaison, Staff Lieutenant Robert "Buck" Dickson, and his two-man guard, a couple of privates named Clark and Ott. A small, whippet-thin guy who looked like he could have run track, Ott seemed almost diminutive beside the thickset Dickson.

Although Dickson and Lillyman had stood over sand tables together at briefings, and Dickson's team wore the Pathfinder wing patch, they hadn't gone through the special training and were somewhat grudgingly accepted by the men who'd done so. Upon making landfall, Dickson and his team were to break off from Lillyman's group on classified orders from regimental headquarters. The S-2s weren't under Lillyman's direct command, and their objective was separate from that of the Pathfinders. He wouldn't be responsible for them once they hit the ground.

As he settled in after embarkation, Lillyman had ample time to ponder his own mission. The transport looped around the airfield for almost two hours—some of the paratroopers were told this was done to throw off possible German observers—before it left the English coast behind. Then, at about 11:30 P.M., it finally stopped circling and soared off over the Channel.

Lieutenant Crouch had a reputation for possessing a cool demeanor behind the controls, and tonight it was in complete evidence. His face taut with concentration, eyes sharply alert, he flew in radio silence, dropping beneath one hundred feet to thwart enemy radar—so close to the water that the troopers nearest their open cabin door could feel the sea spray whipped up by the aircraft's propellers. Had the plane been any lower, it might have clipped the masts of the Allied invasion ships.

Behind him in the troop section, Captain Lillyman glanced out at the naval armada massed below. Destroyers, cruisers, troop carriers, battleships, gunships . . . they seemed to form a floating bridge that stretched on without end. He could practically imagine walking clear across to France on their decks.

One thing was obvious—the water was anything but calm. A strong wind was blowing over the wave tops, tossing ships about in the chop. Depending on variables like gusts and direction, Lillyman knew the wind could cause a slew of problems for the jump. If the men were dispersed over a wider area than expected, it could prevent them from assembling as planned and put them in very dangerous situations.

They didn't speak much throughout the forty-five-minute flight. Their exchanges were short, clipped, and perfunctory. Smoking was barred once they were over the Channel, and most of them abided by the prohibition; they'd been told something about the exhaust from the engines possibly blowing back into the cabin and combusting because of the smokes. Though the risk seemed tiny compared to the dangers they would soon be facing, they'd by and large kept the cigarettes in their pockets.

Some of the men were surprised to find themselves growing drowsy in spite of their nervousness. They felt oddly dull, as if their emotions had been slowed down, and more than a few quietly wondered if it was due to the airsickness tablets they'd been issued before takeoff. The pills came in little cardboard boxes that Sergeant Ray "Snuffy" Smith, the medic, dispensed to them on orders from his regimental superior. While a fair number of the troopers just tossed the pills away, others swallowed them. The contents of the pills, and their distribution to the troopers by the Army, would later draw a number of questions.

Overall the mood aboard the flight was tense. With their bulky gear making it hard to move, the men sat very still in their seats, squeezed together on either side of the troop compartment, butterflies fluttering in their stomachs. The 101st Pathfinders liked to think of themselves as supermen, the toughest of the tough. But as they faced one another across the aisle, their gazes would occasionally meet, and their hardened facades crack a little, each man recognizing his own nervous fear in his comrade's eyes.

The staff sergeant from Headquarters who'd delivered their mission briefing back in England, Hugh Nibley, had asked repeatedly whether they had any questions, and they had raised their hands one after another, slowly, almost tentatively, everyone wanting to know the same thing from him: did they have any chance of survival?

The soft-spoken, articulate Nibley, a former missionary, historical scholar, and intelligence specialist, had given his replies in careful, measured tones. He felt a profound compassion for the men and refused to mislead them with double-talk and false optimism. He praised their courage and unique training, emphasized their preparedness for the mission, and mentioned the support they would have once the invasion force arrived. But the words that left his mouth hadn't contained any more reassurance than the sorrowful look in his eyes as they moved from one young face to another. When the men had asked him their questions, he had seen the bravado drop away from their faces like the paper Mardi Gras masks people held up on sticks.

If nothing else, the Pathfinders had appreciated the sergeant's honesty. They had confidence in their ability to accomplish their mission, but accepted that they didn't have a prayer of coming home alive. Although official post-combat reports would describe them joining in battle songs on the transports, their few halfhearted attempts at singing had quickly petered off into silence, and the noise of the engines had been far too loud for them to hear one another's voice anyway.

In his seat near the rear of the compartment, Dickson felt anxious and out of place. Only three weeks before he'd been coaching the regimental football team, a far cry from his current assignment. But with D-Day's approach he'd been given his high-priority objective and rushed through jump training. Now the tall, broad-shouldered former varsity athlete noticed flashing green lights in the English Channel and wondered aloud about their purpose.

"It's a rescue ship," said one of the Pathfinders in a tone that was almost *too* flat. "Just in case."

Years afterward, Dickson would find out they weren't rescue ships at all, but a pair of Royal Navy patrol guide boats leading Crouch's planes across the Channel with their navigational lights. It would leave him to wonder if the trooper had been pulling his leg or just mistaken. But his deadpan response and the water spraying in the door would always stand out in Dickson's memory of the crossing.

Later, as the C-47 passed over the Channel Islands and made its hard left turn for France, he noted a big German searchlight sweeping the sky, probing for the arrival of the Allied planes.

It was not a comforting sight.

4.

The Cotentin Peninsula on the French seaside jutted into the Channel at the western end of the Allies' amphibious landing area, codenamed Utah Beach. The 101st Airborne had been tasked with capturing four roads between Saint-Martin-de-Varreville and Pouppeville, blowing their smaller bridges and seizing two of the major ones. The 82nd Airborne was to secure the Douve River and crossings at La Fière and Chef du Pont on opposite sides of the Merderet River, establishing a defensive line west of the Merderet. A glider infantry unit of the British 6th Airborne was to take Pegasus Bridge, a drawbridge spanning the Caen Canal.

Together these groups were to block off German reinforcements heading down to the beachhead from the north, simultaneously opening passages for Allied armor and infantry to roll into the French mainland. If they failed to secure these junctures, the American 4th Infantry Division coming ashore at Utah would likely get trapped there on the dunes or bogged down in the flooded Cotentin wetlands—a disaster in either case.

Frank Lillyman's 101st Pathfinder team had departed England shortly before the 82nd Airborne's teams, which were led by Captain Neal McRoberts of the 505th PIR. Along with the American units, two sticks from the British 6th Airborne—it was at their Pathfinder school at RAF North Witham in Lincolnshire that the Americans had trained under Lieutenant Crouch's command— were being sent to mark off the glider landing zones near Pegasus Bridge.

It was up to Lillyman and his men to mark Drop Zone A at the northern edge of the main attack—within six miles of Pouppeville. Meanwhile, two other teams would land nearby at DZs C, D, and E. In his approach to the Cotentin, Lieutenant Crouch had taken an aerial corridor that would run between the German-occupied Guernsey and Alderney Islands, then cross the peninsula's west coast before delivering the Pathfinders to their destinations. But as he neared the shoreline, the veteran pilot saw a thick bank of clouds and fog ahead of him. Blotting out the moonlight, it appeared to reach to an altitude of about three thousand feet.

That immediately threatened to derail Crouch's plan. The transports had been instructed to maintain visual contact until they were over the peninsula, where they would veer off toward their separate drop and landing zones. But once they entered the clouds, it would be impossible to stay in formation or see all the landmarks needed for accurate orientation. Moreover, he could not expect the troopers to jump blindly into the overcast. Their safety was paramount to him.

He thought hard about what action to take, drawing on long years of experience. Like other United Airlines pilots of his era, he'd learned to fly—and navigate—from the great old transcontinental airmail pilots who'd blazed the trail for commercial aviation. The stringent standards he'd set for himself and his IX Troop Carrier Command Pathfinder pilots far exceeded Air Corps requirements—as did his training techniques. Back in England, he'd deliberately confused navigators by recalibrating their instruments so they would have to rely on their eyes and intuition, and had once offered a cash reward and furlough to the crew that could drop a dummy parachutist closest to its target area.

With the cloud stack looming in front of him now, Crouch made a decision to fly in under its bottom layer. Although going in low would make him an easier target for antiaircraft guns, he saw no other acceptable course. Not if he was to give the paratroopers their best shot.

His hands steady on the controls, Crouch shed altitude, dropping well below five hundred feet. The strict radio silence edict had not allowed him to notify the rest of the troop carriers of his intentions, and he only hoped they would see his formation lights clearly enough to follow his lead. Once beneath the mass of clouds, Crouch made a sharp ninety-degree turn inland, throttled back to his 120mph jump speed, and flashed the red standby light beside the cabin door.

Four minutes from the DZ, he held the plane slow and steady.

Beside him, his copilot, Captain Vito Pedone, gazed down at the moonlit terrain below in silence. *How did I get here?* he thought, thankful they hadn't yet come under fire from German antiaircraft batteries.

Pedone, a twenty-one-year-old native New Yorker, had flown twenty-five previous missions with the Air Corps. But this felt almost surreal. When you'd just gone over the English Channel and made the left turn that would take you into Nazi-occupied France, and you were, moreover, helping to fly the lead plane of the invasion, you knew you were part of something different, and understood how much hinged on your success. But you didn't know—couldn't possibly know—what was going to happen.

Still, he told himself, there was no time to be scared. If you were afraid, you might as well get right out of the stinking airplane and go back to base. You had to take control of your senses, think about the people in your plane, and do what was expected of you.

Back in the cabin, meanwhile, Frank Lillyman had been hunkered down on one knee, peering out the jump door and comparing what he saw to aerial photos of the drop zone that he'd memorized before the mission. Like the pilots, he'd been familiarized with important landmarks.

Then he saw the red light blink on and rose to his feet, ordering his men do the same. Although heavily encumbered with gear, they weren't wearing their bulky reserve chutes. It was standard procedure for them to climb aboard the plane with the packed reserves across their midsections, but Williams had asked for permission to remove his, and Lillyman had remained flexible and given it to him. He would place his trust in the private's ability and experience, and his own common sense, over blind adherence to the rule book. If a trooper's main chute failed to deploy at their low jump altitude, he'd be smacking into the ground before the backup could inflate.

After Williams got the go-ahead to shuck his reserve, most of his comrades followed suit—none more happily than Sergeant Smith. Besides his first-aid supplies and plasma bag, the twenty-year-old Kentuckian, who'd enlisted at sixteen without graduating high school, was carrying a fifty-five-pound Eureka radio transmitter. Ridding himself of the spare parachute meant one less heavy item of gear.

Now the troopers rose and went through their preparations, their discarded reserves pushed back under their seats. At Lillyman's command to "Snap up!" they clipped their static lines—the cords that would connect their chutes to the aircraft—to an anchor cable running the length of the cabin. Their hurried equipment checks followed at once, each man inspecting the chute of the man in front of him and yelling out his okay.

Lillyman's final order of business before the jump was to go down the line and make sure the men's static lines were securely attached to the cable. Then he returned to the door to wait.

In the cockpit, Crouch and Pedone felt encouraged by the continued absence of antiaircraft fire, taking it as an indication that they'd surprised the enemy. But they'd missed some landmarks because of the thick ground fog, and it was already midnight before Pedone realized that they were over the village of Saint-Germain-de-Varreville—a mile and a half from their scheduled DZ.

Crouch could not risk getting any farther away from it.

At 12:12 A.M. by his stopwatch, he flipped the switch for the green ready light.

In the troop cabin, Lillyman and his men shuffled toward the exit.

5.

The second team of Pathfinders had been headed for Drop Zone C outside Hiesville, several miles southeast of Team A's goal. Their pilot, Captain Clyde Taylor, had trailed closely behind Crouch's C-47, his eyes on its pale blue wing lights and the faint glow of the flame suppressors on its engine exhausts. But Taylor and his copilot, Lieutenant Hal Sperber, would not enjoy the element of surprise that gave the lead aircraft a reprieve from ground fire.

Shortly after they overflew the Guernsey and Alderney Islands—near the spot where Buck Dickson had noticed enemy searchlights—they lost sight of Crouch's flight group and headed directly into the cloud bank. Peering out the windscreen, they searched for the planes ahead of them, but visibility was so poor they couldn't even see their blue formation lights. It was as if Crouch's V had disappeared, swallowed up by clouds and darkness.

Taylor knew his crew was on its own. Without any other recourse, he trimmed altitude, banked toward his team's DZ, and flashed the ready light.

The paratroopers had no sooner stood up than the sky around the transport lit with red, blue, and green tracers, the pyrotechnics streaking across the night like ribbons of multicolored fire. Almost spellbound, the men stared out at this brilliant display with a mixture of fear and awe. It was as if all the Fourth of Julys in their collective memories had been rolled into one—but these weren't harmless fireworks meant to thrill parents and kids at the town celebration. Their sole purpose was to help the enemy pinpoint the American aircraft's location.

Sergeant Charles Malley was standing in the door when the warning bell clanged through the troop compartment. His wide-eyed attention abruptly shifted from the tracers to the wing of the plane. A loud explosion had shaken the airship; its left engine had been hit and was burning fiercely, trailing flames and smoke.

Taylor and Sperber knew they wouldn't be able to stay in the air long, and that their only hope was to make it back to the Channel for a water landing. Acting at once, Taylor feathered the propeller, moving it parallel to the airflow to increase the plane's gliding distance. Then he banked hard to the right to start his turn. Beside him, Sperber peered out his window and abruptly realized that turn was about to take them straight into another flight in their serial—Plane 5, piloted by Lieutenant Dwight Kroesch. His fingers tightly gripping the yoke, Sperber pushed it forward to bring down the aircraft's nose. It dipped below the other plane in the nick of time, barely avoiding a collision that would have turned both of them into aerial fireballs.

Taylor, meanwhile, had gotten on the intercom and issued hurried instructions to his crew chief, Marvin Blackburn, who was back in the troop section with the paratroopers. At the door, Sergeant Malley heard him shout above the loud ringing of the bell, repeatedly giving an emergency jump order: *"Clear the ship! Clear the ship! Clear the ship!"*

Malley didn't budge from where he stood. After staring downward for an endless moment, he turned to Lieutenant Gordon Rothwell, his jumpmaster and the leader of Pathfinder Team C.

"Hold!" he shouted, motioning at the bushy treetops. The trees were so close to the belly of the aircraft, Malley almost felt that he could reach down to touch them with his hands. *"Hold the men!"*

Rothwell understood at once. The plane had dropped too low on its remaining engine. It would be suicidal for the troopers to bail. Their chutes would have no time to deploy before they hit the trees.

He ordered them to wait. Antiaircraft rounds riddled the floor of the fuselage, whizzing through the troop section. Pressed together in its dim, tight confines, their apprehensive faces starkly limned by the tracers, the men mouthed silent prayers—hard, serious prayers—and awaited further orders.

At the controls, Taylor pulled the transport's nose sharply upward amid the volleys of tracer and AA fire coming from below. Then Sperber appeared from the cockpit. "Everything overboard!" he called out. "We're going down!"

His heart pounding in his chest, Lieutenant Taylor had swung hard back toward the Channel. The plane was as good as lost, and if he crashed into the trees, so were the men onboard. Their only chance at survival would be a water landing.

In the troop section, the Pathfinders felt their stomachs flip-flop as the plane reversed course. They were hurriedly shedding ballast, jettisoning everything that wasn't essential or bolted in place. Bringing out their knives, they began cutting themselves free of parachute harnesses, backpacks, leg bags, and gun straps—there wasn't a moment to waste undoing buckles or clips. Weapons went out the door, as did ammunition. Fitted with explosive mechanisms to prevent them from falling into enemy hands, the cutting-edge Eureka radar units also suddenly became expendable. Malley would recall pulling the detonator cord on one before he hoisted it through the exit—and moments later accidentally cutting one of his mates through to his rib section while slashing off his harness.

The man winced in pain, blood soaking through his uniform. Although Malley would joke about having earned him a Purple Heart, he'd known it was anything but a laughing matter when it happened. If the wound had hampered his ability swim, he might well have been a goner.

But there had been no time for either of them to think. Blackburn was back in the tumult of the cabin, shouting for everyone to jump, telling them they were going to hit the water.

Jump hell, Malley thought. Most of the troopers had already cut themselves out of their chutes and stripped down to their boots and combat uniforms. What was he talking about? How were they supposed to jump?

The plane rattled around them as it accelerated, a shuddering vibration the men could feel deep in their bones. All they could do now was get ready to ditch.

Struggling to control their fear, the soldiers fell back on their training and hastily shrugged into yellow Mae West life vests, pulling the cords to inflate them. Then they got down on the floor of the cabin, facing the rear of the transport, each trooper with his legs bracketing the man in front of him. Rothwell was the only exception; as jumpmaster, he was responsible for trying to inflate the dinghies. If the men survived the landing, they would need them to stay alive.

Their descent gathered speed, a red flare searing the darkness outside the plane. Low above the Channel now, Taylor had released it to illuminate the water's roiling surface.

Suddenly he brought up the aircraft's nose, making every effort to belly into the sea and distribute the force of collision. As the plane's tail angled downward, the men braced for impact, sweating nervously, their pulses quickening, some with their heads bowed in silent prayer.

Finally the transport smacked into the Channel with a loud, wrenching crump, tossing the men about the cabin.

After that there was nothing around them but water.

6.

In Crouch's lead plane, Bluford Williams had abruptly noticed some confusion up front near the door. He didn't know how long it had been since Lillyman ordered the men to jump with a hollered "*Let's go!*" It could have been a minute, or several minutes. He couldn't tell. His sense of time had been washed away in a heady rush of adrenaline.

Standing at the end of the stick, he'd risen from his aluminum seat prepared to nudge along anybody who lagged or froze up with sudden hesitation. But that didn't seem to be the problem. From where he stood, it appeared that one of the guys—Mangoni, he thought—had gotten his rifle hung on the edge of the door.

The M-1s were supposed to be broken down and carried in a heavy padded leg case called a Griswold bag, but none of the troopers had been able to figure out who was responsible for that idea. Surely, they'd complained, it was some genius who'd never jumped from a height of five feet, let alone five hundred. Like their other leg bags, which had been invented by the Brits for their own airborne forces, the Griswolds were ungainly impediments to movement.

Most of the men had chosen to jump without one of them, just as they'd decided against using their reserve chutes. Instead, they had kept their fully assembled rifles tucked under their harness straps, where they could reach for them quickly after making landfall.

Lillyman had given his tacit approval by turning a blind eye, even knowing there was a risk involved: the wind would tear at them when they dropped, sweeping off whatever gear wasn't properly secured. But he was a combat officer, not a pencil pusher, and he understood the situations his troopers would face on the ground. When a soldier came down in hostile territory with enemy soldiers shooting at him, the last thing he wanted was to squander precious seconds reassembling his M-1. Taking fire without a functional weapon in hand was a far deadlier prospect than getting momentarily caught in the jump door.

Still, Mangoni had gotten his rifle snagged, or so Williams would recall. Dickson, the S-2 commander from regimental HQ, thought one of the paratroopers, saddled with a heavy load of equipment, had tripped over one of his leg bags and lost his balance. Neither of them had the clearest view from where they stood, but it was undebatable that somebody was having problems. In the commotion, Lillyman stepped out of position to help him.

Then McFarlen felt a hand on his back, urging him toward the door. The plane was already making its pass of the DZ and in moments would turn back toward home. There wasn't time to think or hesitate. He would no longer be the third man to exit the transport, but the first.

The troopers had wanted to use the jump cry "Geronimo" after cooking it up to match their Indian warrior haircuts. But it would have to wait for another time. The ailing General William C. Lee was commander of the 101st, and the father of the U.S. Army airborne. In the days before the invasion, it had gotten around that the troopers would honor him by calling out his name instead.

McFarlen remembered that as he moved into the doorway and gazed down at the fog-shrouded Normandy countryside, his ears filling with the merged thunder of the wind, the aircraft's engines, and his own savagely beating heart.

"Bill Lee!" he shouted into the void.

And leaped.

7.

Coming down with their landing lights on, Captain Taylor and his copilot, Harold Sperber, had at first seen only water in front of them, bright green in the moonlight. Then, suddenly, the huge form of a ship. Steeling himself against the worst, Taylor wrenched at his control column and managed to turn away from yet another deadly collision.

The plane hit the Channel hard. Cold seawater came surging up around it in a great wave, gushing through the door of its troop section. Taylor's expert landing had kept the plane intact, but it was flooding fast.

"Get the troops out, this baby's going down!"

It was Sperber shouting into the troop section this time, poking his head down from the aircraft's astrodome, the glass observation bubble above and behind its cockpit. Meant for celestial navigation, it had now become a crow's nest from which he could scan for nearby vessels. But in those first moments after the crash, he saw neither friendly nor hostile ships around him. There was only the darkness on all sides.

Below him in the cabin, the men were now knee-deep in freezing water. They stood up off the riveted metal floor, their soaked uniform trousers clinging to their legs, their skin prickled with gooseflesh. Lieutenant Rothwell and several others were furiously pushing the dinghies out the door, trying to get the men who couldn't swim onto them ahead of the rest. But the lieutenant had not been able to inflate more than a few of the rafts, and the current was sweeping them away faster than anyone could haul himself inside.

Sloshing toward the exit, Malley noticed that Private First Class Steve Pustola's pockets were bulging with service pistols. He'd stuffed them full of the Colt .45s as they'd been passed up the line of paratroopers to be tossed overboard. A Brooklyn boy, Pustola had a thing for those guns. He never seemed to have enough of them, and, sink or swim, he'd been intent on hanging on to as many as he could. But Malley had heard that people from Brooklyn were all a little bit crazy.

One of the men crowding at the door, Private First Class Richard M. Wright—his flame-colored hair had earned him the nickname "Red" with his teammates—was simultaneously grateful and disappointed. Grateful he was still alive, disappointed that he'd been shot down before the jump. Wright hated the brutality and carnage of war. Hated the death and the killing. But he'd paid close attention to what was happening in Europe since Hitler's ascent to power and had come to hate the evil of Nazi tyranny more than anything on earth.

Though warned it was tantamount to committing suicide, Red had volunteered for Pathfinder duty with his close friends Terrence "Salty" Harris and Dutch Fenstermaker, figuring it was the quickest way to join the fight. That wasn't to be, not now, not for him and Dutch, who was a member of his stick. But Harris was on Plane Number 5, the transport right behind theirs, and Wright hoped he'd make it to Normandy.

As he prepared to swim out the door, Red swore he'd still get into the war somehow. . . . *if he survived the night.* In his mind, it was by no means a certainty. The plane was sinking in a hurry, and the sea around it might be teeming with enemy patrol boats. Wright knew it was possible he'd drown before anyone, the Germans or the Allies, fished him out of the water.

Taking a deep gulp of air, he splashed out into the Channel, swimming away from the plane to avoid being dragged down with it. He could discern the bobbing forms of his comrades in the brilliant glow of the moon, hear them calling to each other as they struggled to keep their heads above the swells. Beyond a few feet away, he saw nothing around him. No lights, no ships, nothing.

Then he heard some of the men shouting that they'd located one of the dinghies. He swam in its direction, guided by their voices.

"This way . . . this way . . . over here!"

Wright's arms and legs were almost numb from the cold when he got to the raft. He grabbed its edge and saw hands reach down from onboard to clutch at his uniform and Mae West, hoisting him up and in. At last he rolled over the side, catching his breath. There were two or three others on the dinghy with him, all shivering and drenched in briny water. A lifeline ran from inside the raft, the men in the water gripping every inch of its corded length, its slack fully paid out so it was taut as a bowstring. He felt a surge of relief when he saw Dutch Fenstermaker among them.

Soaking wet from head to toe, his teeth chattering uncontrollably, Wright sat up and peered into the night. The little rubber dinghy couldn't hold any more men than the few already aboard. The evacuees would have to take turns climbing onto it, or those hanging onto the rope would rapidly succumb to exposure.

Time passed, no one knew how much for sure. The men were quiet, trying to conserve energy. Water whipping around it, their transport had reared in the waves like a great gray bird that had plunged seaward in its terminal spasms, then begun to spiral down toward the Channel's shallow bottom.

In the distance, the men heard the drone of planes, the rattle of antiaircraft fire . . . and closer, too close, the sound of the wavelets lapping at the edges of the dinghy. They saw no sign of approaching ships and weren't certain if that was good or bad.

Helpless and battered, drifting alone in enemy waters, they could do nothing but wait to find out.

8.

In the sky behind Taylor's downed transport, the remaining two planes in Team C bore on toward the Hiesville drop zone. Their pilots could only hope and pray the lead flight had ditched without breaking up, and that its crew and passengers had managed to escape serious harm. With German flak guns thumping on the ground and tracers streaking the darkness around them, it was all their aircrews could do to safely deliver the Pathfinders to their target area.

Commanded by Lieutenant Roy Kessler, the troopers on Plane 5 had now become the serial's primary stick. Among that group was Red Wright's buddy Private First Class Salty Harris, who'd gotten his nickname because he'd once attended the Naval Academy, leaving after a series of disciplinary infractions that he would mainly attribute to boredom. Strapping, good-humored, and exuberantly foul-mouthed, Harris had found the atmosphere at Annapolis far too passive for his disposition, and in the end had guessed he just wasn't cut out to be a Navy man. Possessed of a raucous fighting spirit that he attributed to his Irish lineage, he'd wanted action and found it in the Army, where he'd started out with a mortar company and been one of the early volunteers for the paratrooper school in Toccoa, Georgia.

While there with the 506th PIR's Easy Company, Harris met Wright and many of his other closest friends—in fact, he'd sat next to Wright on the bus to Toccoa and they'd hit it off right away. At paratrooper school, he'd trained under Captain Herbert Sobel, known to the men as the "Black Swan," a notorious disciplinarian whose methods were considered unnecessarily harsh by the majority of his recruits. Making staff sergeant in a hurry, Harris would become as respected among the troopers of Easy Company as Sobel was despised and resented—a kind of accessible, everyman yin to the Black Swan's stiffly detached yang.

Just weeks before Normandy, the men's gaining frustration with the captain came to a boil with his revocation of their three-day passes over a minor incident. At the center of a protest against Sobel that got him busted in rank, Harris was transferred out of Easy without being allowed to pick up his bags. He hadn't been inclined to complain; it was better than the court-martial for mutiny he'd barely dodged—and, on the flip side, also better than he would have felt if he'd stood by and done nothing about Sobel. No one would have denied that E Company was a crackerjack outfit, a model for the paratroop infantry—and that Sobel deserved credit for helping to whip it into shape. But the captain had demoralized Easy's enlisted men even as they'd needed to muster their confidence for the coming invasion. Harris and several of his fellow noncoms had felt him to be almost sadistic in the punishments he doled out for the most minor breaches of discipline—and in their eyes, his behavior had become more and more irrational as the prospect of jumping into battle had ground on his nerves. In the end, they grew convinced he'd been unfit to lead men into combat and was bound to get them unnecessarily killed.

If Harris still dwelled on the episode on the eve of D-Day, he kept it to himself. When one of his old Easy platoon commanders had recruited him for the Pathfinder school, he'd eagerly seized the chance. He didn't care that it was pegged a landing spot for screwups and agitators, or that that was probably the main reason he'd been asked to volunteer. Nor did he care that they were supposedly training for a mission of no return. Figuring he'd deal with whatever the mission might be when he had to, Harris had simply decided Pathfinder duty would give him a fresh start, get him into the thick of the action he craved, and keep him together with some of his closest friends in Easy Company. Dick Wright and Carl "Dutch" Fenstermaker had been steered toward the Pathfinders mainly *because* they were his friends, and both were now aboard Plane 4. Mike Ranny, who had gotten into trouble with Harris during the Sobel incident, also took the special signal training at North Witham, but he'd rejoined Easy when the opening came up.

Whatever Harris was thinking as his flight approached the DZ, he kept it to himself. He likely had no inkling that Wright and Fenstermaker's plane had gotten shot out of the air—the flight crew wouldn't have rushed to share that information—and was focused on his particular responsibilities. Kessler had entrusted him with carrying and rigging one of the stick's two radar homing beacons, which said everything about how highly he was regarded by the CO. While the light panels were important visual aids for the squadrons flying to Drop Zone C, eighty-one planeloads of airborne infantry were relying heavily on the Eureka sets to bring them in from a distance of twenty miles. Aboard the cockpits of the C-47s, transponder units called Rebecca interrogators would send out timed radar pulses that, upon finding the Eureka beacons on the ground, would be rebroadcast to the Rebeccas on a different frequency and picked up by directional antennas mounted on the planes. It was no coincidence, then, that the word *eureka* was Greek for "I have found it."

Now the red signal light blinked, and Lieutenant Kessler gave the orders to stand up and hook up. Harris pushed to his feet and began his equipment checks. Back in England, he'd been called a disgrace to the company he'd helped found, and had the stripes he'd proudly earned at Toccoa peeled from his shoulders. But now he'd be able to show his worth where it counted, on the battlefield. It would be, if not redemption, then a kind of validation for him.

The green light came on. Salty Harris moved into the aisle, and then was standing in the open doorway. His team's pilot, Lieutenant Dwight Kroesch, had opted to fly in above rather than under the clouds and had given the go signal at a higher altitude than many of the other flights. Seen in the moonlight, the French

34

countryside below Harris would have resembled a relief map, or one of the sand table dioramas he'd seen at the pre-mission brief-ings. But there had been neither tracers nor belching antiaircraft guns coming from those scale models.

He had wanted action and gotten his wish. The enemy defenses were awake and spitting fire up into the sky.

Ready as any man could be, he jumped into their vicious teeth.

9.

Minutes earlier, Captain Frank Lillyman's team had learned a practical benefit of jumping from a very low altitude: It didn't leave them with time to think about their vulnerability, feel the bottoms drop out of their stomachs as gravity hauled them downward, or for that matter think or feel much of anything at all. The experi-ence passed so quickly it was a blur. There was the prop blast whip-ping them toward the C-47's tail, the shock of their chutes blossoming open and jerking their harnesses up into their crotches, and then, about twenty-five seconds after they left the aircraft, the ground racing up to meet them.

The men had been taught to control the drops with their canvas risers—the straps that connected to the shroud lines running up to the canopy. If a trooper pulled his left front riser, he would turn left. If he pulled the right riser, he'd float over in that direction. If he pulled both of them at the same time he would accelerate his descent, spilling air from the front of his chute. The harder he pulled, the more air he released in the appropriate section of the canopy, and when he pulled hard enough the canopy would deflate to allow for his landing.

Simple in theory, but a paratrooper's abilities were honed through innumerable tower drills, dozens of jumps out of flying aircraft, and many months of arduous physical fitness training for strength, stamina, and coordination. The Pathfinders, moreover, had gone through an additional level of intensive preparation at North Witham, where they were trained to set up and operate the special equipment they would bring behind enemy lines.

Descending quickly, Lillyman sailed over the treetops and tugged on his forward risers, convinced the open field below would be a good place to land. His chin tucked low, knees slightly bent, he went into a practiced sideways roll as the chute collapsed with a fluttery whisper and then poured to the ground in a loose heap.

His landing accomplished, he scrambled to his feet and shucked his harness. The stogie was still jutting from his teeth, a good indication his luck would be holding up.

But not all the signs were that reassuring. Even as the full realization that he was on enemy ground sank in, Lillyman realized he was alone in the field. He heard bursts of machine-gun fire an uncertain distance away, saw 40mm tracers flaring like otherworldly lightning above the treetops. But there was neither sight nor sound of his men or their security detail. For some reason—he conjectured it was the delayed jumps when Mangoni got fouled up in the plane—the troopers seemed to have been widely scattered across the area. With Crouch flying about 110 miles an hour, a half minute's holdup for Mangoni would have resulted in the men behind him jumping hundreds of yards from those who'd preceded him out the door.

Lillyman continued to evaluate his situation, his hands automatically dropping to his carbine. The field looked different from the ones he'd seen in the sand table diagrams and reconnaissance photos. Much smaller, for one thing. He'd known about the hedgerows bordering the peninsula's roads and farmlands. But the growth around the pasture was closer to fifty feet high than the fifteen his briefings had led him to expect. The foliage looked old, even ancient, each hedge a wildly overgrown jumble of shrubs, trees, and roots. They seemed almost impassable to him at first glance.

He was trying to orient himself, figure out where he was relative to the DZ, when he heard a sound across the field. Something had moved in the darkness at its edge, near a tall, tangled line of bushes. The breath catching in his throat, he turned his gun toward the noise. His orders were to do no shooting, to avoid betraying his position. He was supposed to be a ghost, a phantom stealing through the night, taking evasive action if he encountered enemy forces. Unless he had no other choice.

A moment or two passed. Biting into his cigar, his eyes narrow and alert in his camo-smeared face, Lillyman peered across the field and turned his M-1 toward the sound.

Then whatever he'd heard parted with the shadows and moved toward him—a slow, lumbering shape much too large and bulky to be human.

Lillyman slid his finger over his rifle's trigger . . . and then suddenly heard a low, deep *moo*. His windpipe unlocking, the breath streaming from his mouth, he lowered the weapon and grinned. The cow trudged slowly over to where he stood, stuck out her big, moist, fleshy nose, and snuffled the sleeve of his jump jacket.

He looked at the beast, flushed with relief. Thanks to her, he felt about five years older than he had a few minutes ago.

When the newspapers and radios blare out the news, remember that your pappy led the way. He'd written those words to Jane in mid-May, right after he was briefed about his Pathfinders' role in the coming invasion, but hadn't supposed his first encounter on enemy-held soil would be with a cow. It would be a story worth telling her sometime.

Right now, though, Lillyman had to find his men. If he was going to do that, he'd have to retrace Crouch's flight path. They would have been scattered along that line.

With a silent good-bye to this bovine welcomer, he checked his wrist compass and went sprinting across the pasture toward an opening in the hedges, as alone as he'd felt in his entire life.

10.

At about half past midnight, Captain Basil T. Jones, the skipper of the HMS *Tartar*, found himself staring straight into the jaws of a major conundrum. Assigned picket duty off the west coast of the Cotentin Peninsula, his 377-foot Tribal-class destroyer was the flagship of the British Royal Navy's 10 Destroyer Flotilla, a group

on patrol against enemy vessels that might be attempting to inter-
cept the Allied landing forces or resupply German troops on the
beachhead.

Jones's orders were to stop for nothing unless it was to engage
the enemy. The admiralty had been clear about that. They wanted
to ensure that his group was undistracted, and to minimize any
chance of Nazi vessels slipping through its line of defense.

But just minutes ago, every sailor on *Tartar*'s deck had spotted an
aircraft plunging out of the sky within yards of the destroyer, its left
wing engulfed in ragged orange flames. Her lookouts had almost
immediately witnessed men bailing out of the plane into the Channel. Notified over the ship's telephone, Captain Jones had instructed
his steersmen to investigate and hurried topside for a firsthand look.
When he reached the upper deck, the destroyer's searchlights were
beaming through the misty darkness toward the downed, sinking
aircraft. Several men were hollering over the gunwales and waving
toward a nearby lifeboat in the water. A relatively new crew that had
come on board following a major refit in January, the sailors had
seen little combat to this point and were excited and anxious.

"*They're Jerries!*"

"*Shoot the bastards!*"

Raising his binoculars to his eyes, Jones heard shouts coming
back at them across the heaving water: "Ship ahoy! We're American paratroopers! *American paratroopers!*"

Jones knew he had a decision to make. Obviously, the men
clinging to that raft could not be friend and foe at the same time.

He peered through the goggles, shifting his focus between the
survivors and their sinking plane. The aircraft's nose and wings were
almost submerged, but he was able to see its rear section projecting

out of the water like the tail of a breaching whale. Steadying the binoculars on that part of the fuselage, the skipper identified horizontal white bands near its tail wings—the distinct markings of an Allied invasion plane.

Jones thought hard now. He was a veteran forty-three-year-old officer and nobody's fool. In the weeks leading up to D-Day, SHAEF had issued repeated warnings about German efforts at deception and infiltration. While all those men surviving a plunge from the sky could have been viewed as a happy miracle, the captain couldn't have been faulted if he'd been suspicious of what he saw, or even felt it an impossible strain on his credibility. As a flotilla commander, he bore a grave responsibility for the safety of four warships and their crews. He needed to be cautious.

But caution was only part of the matter for Jones. The rest was the simple nature of his mission. HMS *Tartar* was not a search-and-rescue ship. He'd received strict instructions to keep the ship on patrol, to stop for nothing unless it was to engage an enemy vessel. Under the circumstances, he would be justified in simply radioing a message to the fleet about the men in the water, thereby making them someone else's problem. In fact, it would be a full-out violation of orders if he stopped to pick them up.

But the drink was rough tonight, and freezing cold, and it looked as if more than a score of the men were desperately trying to hang on to a single lifeboat. What if no one came to pull them out? The Germans had threatened to shoot Allied paratroopers as spies, without regard for the Geneva accords. If they were indeed who they claimed to be—and this was, after all, the American invasion sector—the enemy might discover them in the water and pick them off like ducks in a pond.

Captain Jones stirred all these factors together and then weighed them, searching his heart and conscience. Mindful that orders were orders, he could really do just one thing.

Soberly, he gave his command. The decision hadn't taken him long. Right or wrong, he would have to live with it.

11.

If the irony of Private Ray "Snuffy" Smith's predicament even occurred to him, it would have been a fleeting awareness. Once down on enemy soil, the Pathfinders were to a man living in the moment, propelled from one to the next by the dual imperatives of their mission and basic survival. He would have had other things on his mind.

But whatever he may or may not have thought about his mishap, it was a wicked turn of fate. He was the team's medic. His job was to tend to their wounded. Yet he was the first in his unit to be injured, breaking his foot on landfall.

Nicknamed after the popular cartoon character Snuffy Smith— a moonshining hillbilly who shared Ray's deep Southern-Appalachian accent and boisterous personality—the twenty-year-old Kentuckian had joined the army four years earlier after quitting high school, then trained as a medical corpsman with the 4th Infantry at Fort Benning, Georgia, and been promoted to sergeant by the time he was seventeen. A natural as a medic, he'd been handpicked for the Medical Corps officer training program, only to be disqualified when his paperwork revealed he hadn't gotten past the eighth grade. Stung and disappointed by the rejection, Smith had volunteered for paratrooper school, knowing full well it would mean getting bumped down to private. But the parachute pay was fifty dollars a month better than the average enlisted man's wage, and, besides, he'd wanted in on the action.

After he earned his wings, the Pathfinder units put out a call for medics, and Smith decided to respond. Why not put his training to use where it counted? It had seemed like the way to go.

Carrying the Eureka unit and first-aid supplies tonight, Smith had been among the most overloaded troopers aboard the lead flight. It is no mystery, then, why he was one of the men to jump without the reserve parachute. But he didn't blame his tree landing on the bulky combat load. To him, it was just a nasty fluke.

There had been no problems during the jump. Before clearing the door of the plane, he had looked out and seen nothing but the horizon. There was no incoming flak, no tracer fire. Then he'd felt a push from behind and leaped into the night.

The grove of apple trees had appeared below in a hurry. He'd hurtled down into one of them, unable to get clear of it, twigs and branches tearing at his skin, his chute and static lines getting entangled, leaves flying everywhere, pale green June apples dropping all around him.

Smith's descent finally came to a halt when he found himself dangling from a limb of the tree, suspended by his twisted lines. He'd landed in a churchyard enclosed by a low stone wall and could see the church close by in the moonlight.

Then he noticed the vague silhouettes of helmets about fifty feet away across the grove. Alarmed and helpless, he peered in their direction, knowing he'd be able to recognize German coal scuttles if he got a halfway decent look at them. But despite the brightness of the moon it was too dark to make out the helmet shapes.

With a deep breath, Smith struggled to escape his harness. Whether the soldiers were friend or enemy, he had to get out of the tree . . . but all he accomplished trying to unfasten his straps was to shake more apples from the branches. They rained down amid a flutter of leaves and twigs and then went bouncing off his body to the ground.

Pulling his trench knife out of its boot sheath, Smith cut his shroud lines and dropped among the apples. It was a hard spill, but he quickly discovered that wasn't the worst of it. Something was seriously wrong with his foot. He couldn't rest his weight on it without pain, and it was swelling up fast.

He instantly realized he'd broken a bone, or even suffered a compound fracture. As a medic he knew all the indications, and his weren't good.

Smith knew he couldn't just wait there to be discovered, though. His first order of business was to locate his teammates, and the first step would be to identify the shadowy forms across the churchyard.

He reached into a pocket, fishing for his cricket. Given to every Screaming Eagle before D-Day, the little metal clicking devices were military-issue versions of the novelty toys found in Cracker Jack boxes. Since the cricket would click once when its tab was depressed and a second time when it was released, it had been determined that one set of clicks would be the challenge and a double set the response.

His clicker in hand, using the trees and bushes for cover, Smith crept toward the indistinct forms he'd seen moving about him.

His injured foot felt like a huge swollen lump in his boot. He would need to give himself a shot of morphine if he was going to keep walking on it, and he had no way of telling how well he'd get around even with a hypo. But first things first.

Squatted behind a patch of shrubbery with bated breath, aiming his rifle in the direction of the men, he raised the cricket and snapped it in front of him.

Click-clack.

Thankfully the answering signal came almost at once:

Click-clack, click-clack.

He relaxed and lowered his weapon. It had been a double snap—the correct identifier.

He emerged from the shrubs that had lent him cover. Stepping forward, he could see more than just their American helmets now, and recognized Mangoni and another paratrooper. His foot throbbing badly, he limped over to join them.

Lost, disoriented, and frazzled, the men exchanged very few words as they came together, sharply aware that they needed to get on with their mission. But Smith could barely put pressure on his foot and knew he wouldn't be able to keep up with the others without a painkiller. Nor could they afford to have him slow them down.

He got the morphine syrette out of his kit. It would be too agonizing to take off his boot, so he rolled up his pants and injected the lower part of his leg. That helped a little.

Half-carrying him along between them, aware time was running out, the Pathfinders moved off across the field to search for the rest of their team.

12.

Private Delbert Jones, another of the men to jump from Plane
Number 1, had landed hard in a small courtyard, his helmet scrap-
ing down along its surrounding rock wall. The helmet's metal shell
may have saved his life, and it certainly spared him from a trau-
matic blow to his skull, but the collision had been noisy, and that
wasn't a good thing.

Tumbling to the ground with a grunt, the wind knocked out of
him, he'd lain flat on his back in the darkness for several seconds.
A signal-light man, Jones was so weighted down with equipment
he could hardly move, no less get his Holophanes and other gear
out from under his harness.

Confused, he looked around and saw a rustic stone building
just yards away. A light was on inside it, leaching across the court
from the narrow space under the door.

Jones's brow filmed with sweat. He remembered the sandbox
models showing German barracks at the northern end of the drop
zone—old country farmhouses they'd confiscated for the use of
their troops. It seemed likely he'd fallen outside one of them.

He quickly pulled himself together. If the structure was in fact
a barracks, it would be patrolled by sentries, and the loud clanking
of his helmet against the stone wall could have easily alerted them

to his presence. But he couldn't yield to panic. He would need all his wits about him to avoid enemy soldiers and had only a short while to set up his lights for the paratroopers of the 502nd.

Pushing up to a sitting position, Jones fumbled around under his chest packs until he was able to work open the harness. Then he extricated his carbine and signal lights and rose to his feet. He could only guess at his location, and had no idea where his teammates might be. Somehow, he'd have to gain his bearings and then go find them.

Jones scurried off, hugging the wall, relying on his wrist compass to help him move back along his jump stick's line of dispersal. He searched for an opening, a gate, some way out of the yard. When he couldn't find one, he planted his hands on the wall and boosted himself over the top.

The weight of his packs made him take another stumbling misstep as he came down on the opposite side. Then the night upended and he was once again sprawled on the ground.

When Jones got up, he was surrounded by tombstones. Like the farmhouse from which he'd fled, the cemetery was ages old. Partly surrounded by hedgerows, its burial plots were covered with moss, their cracked, leaning markers bleached chalk-white from exposure to the elements.

Peering across the uneven rows of graves, he saw the outlines of three men near a bordering hedge and froze.

Tensely alert, he stood near the wall in silence as they came closer.

13.

Landing in the same enclosed courtyard as Jones, Frank Rocca had also seen the light under the stone building's front door and guessed that its occupants might be wide awake. But for him there was no mistaking the structure for a farmhouse or German military barracks. As he'd done on the firing range, quickly knocking out human-shaped targets from every angle like he had two sets of eyes, the blocky little private made a snap assessment of his surroundings. In the midst of his descent, he'd seen a high church steeple beyond the wall of the courtyard, a cemetery outside another part of the wall, and determined that the house with the light shining from it was the parsonage.

After he touched down, Rocca had gotten out of his chute rig without a hitch, gathered up his equipment, and leapfrogged over the wall into the adjoining cemetery. There were a lot of places that would have been outwardly more dangerous than a church caretaker's front yard, but he knew the Germans had occupied many local homes, and wasn't eager to alert anyone to his presence.

Although he and Rocca did not encounter each other in the courtyard—Jones may well have left it before Rocca crashed to the ground—the Pathfinders both headed off in the same general direction, seeking to retrace Lieutenant Crouch's flight path and find their brothers.

14.

Mangoni and John Zamanakos had sat elbow-to-elbow aboard the transport and jumped one after the other. But the demolition men had been separated when they landed on different sides of a large hedgerow.

Alone in a tree-studded field, Zamanakos—like Jones—had trouble unbuckling his parachute harness. He'd hooked his Eureka unit under his chest packs and over the harness's straps, and the big piece of equipment had gotten in the way of things. Finally, he had to use his trench knife to cut his risers.

Free of the chute now, he looked this way and that, saw a long, deep ditch running parallel to the hedgerow, and crawled down into it, hoisting his radar unit over the dirt embankment. Then he waited and listened.

For a few moments, he heard nothing but winged insects flittering and buzzing past his ears. Then at last the sounds he'd been hoping for reached him from the near distance: *Click-clack . . . click-clack . . . click-clack . . .*

A cricket.

He took out his own device without leaving the drainage ditch. It offered him more than vital cover; when he'd checked his compass, he seen that it roughly traced his transport's line of flight. Since the other members of his stick also would be heading that way, his path was sure to converge with theirs if he stayed down in it.

Grimed and sweaty, Zamanakos tramped through the ditch with his transmitter box, repeatedly clicking the little signal device in front of him as he moved along. He didn't have much time before the planes appeared from the west seeking the drop zone. However far off it might be, he and his teammates had to get there first to bring them in.

15.

Click-clack . . . click-clack . . .

Click-clack, click-clack . . . click-clack, click-clack . . .

The signals given and received, Jones hurried toward the three shadowy forms across the graveyard. One was Snuffy Smith, the outfit's medic. He'd clearly been injured and was being half-dragged along by the others.

The Pathfinders assembled at the edge of the cemetery and then moved into a neighboring orchard, where more troopers from their flight joined them after hearing their clickers: Mangoni, Rocca, Wilhelm, T/5 Owen Council, and then Zamanakos. His helmet and uniform covered with mud and soil from trekking through the ditch, his face smeared with camo paint, he looked to all eyes around him like he'd clawed his way out of a nearby grave.

Together in the field now, the men hastily compared notes. Though most reported seeing the church and enclosed courtyard, no one had noticed any German soldiers or vehicles around the structure Jones had thought might be a barracks. This led them to agree that it was probably still occupied by the local parson.

Flustered and discombobulated, Wilhelm now shared his own experience of landing in a wood-ringed pasture; spooked by the heavy darkness, he'd nervously turned on his Holophane.

"I wanted to see if it would work," he said, realizing how crazy that must have sounded.

As it turned out, he explained, the panel had done more than "work"—it had lit up the night around him with its brilliant reflectorized glare, startling him out of his momentary confusion and making him realize that he might as well have turned on a neon sign revealing his position to enemy soldiers. Fueled by that thought, he had left the field in a hurry, fortunate not to have alerted every German in the area.

With almost half the stick assembled, the troopers now had to decide how to carry out their orders. They knew they were southeast of Pouppeville, where they were supposed to have dropped—but none of the men were sure how far to the southeast, making it all the more urgent that they not waste a minute. Although Captain Lillyman and the rest of their team were still unaccounted for, they would have to move off toward the DZ without them.

At least with regard to Lillyman, that would prove unnecessary. The entire group breathed a collective sigh of relief when he stepped out of the night with Tom Walton, having met up with him while following all the clicks and clacks. Walton and Council were T/5s, or technician fifth grades, trained at operating the Eureka beacon; with both men present, the group was at last entirely capable of readying a drop zone.

Their big problem was timing. Or more precisely, the amount of time left to them. Lillyman had already determined that the Pathfinders wouldn't be able to reach their assigned DZ before the flights came in, leaving him to present them with a simple contingency plan: namely to get as close to the original location as possible in the minutes they had left and find a field large enough for the 502nd to use as an alternate landing spot. The members of the stick—and security detail—who were still missing when they headed out would hopefully follow in that same direction and catch up to them.

As for Lieutenant Dickson and his men: The S-2s hadn't been seen by anyone since before the jump, but they'd also been last to exit the transport, meaning they would have landed farthest from the troopers closest the door. More important—if cold-blooded— was the realization that their classified mission had nothing to do with preparing the DZ. Wherever Dickson's party had come down, the bottom line was that they were on their own.

Finished with his huddle, Lillyman gave the men a brisk order to move out, Jones slipping an arm under Snuffy Smith's shoulder to help him along, another member of the group relieving the medic of his Eureka. It was obvious to all of them that he was barely able to stand up on his own, let alone carry the weighty instrument.

Their course of action set, the Pathfinders hastened northeast across the fields, looking for a suitable place to lay out their beacons.

16.

About six weeks before the invasion, in mid-May, the U.S. military's G2 Intelligence Corps had begun noticing tiny black specks on their aerial surveillance photos of projected drop zones across the Cotentin Peninsula. The number of specks multiplied daily and were soon identified as vertical wooden poles spaced between seventy-five and a hundred yards apart, with cables strung between them in a way that they could shred alighting Allied gliders to pieces and kill or maim descending paratroopers on landfall. Fabricated out of logs and railroad ties, they would become known as "Rommel's asparagus" after the German field marshal who'd masterminded the Atlantic defenses and ordered them planted in the ground like the vegetables they resembled. Spied among them outside the farming hamlet of Saint-Martin-de-Varreville were two buildups of casemented 105mm howitzers, and parking bays for military vehicles—including heavy armor.

The poles were so numerous and easily replaceable that little could be done about them. But the heavy guns were another story. They presented a grave threat to the ships bringing men and supplies ashore on Utah Beach, making them prime targets of the 502nd PIR's airborne troops. In fact, regimental HQ was convinced that "the fate of the northern half of the operation could have turned" on whether the coastal batteries were taken out before the arrival of the amphibious assault waves.

Destroying the batteries would be a challenge for two main reasons, however: The Allies were unfamiliar with the local roads leading up to them, and many of those roads had been deliberately flooded by the Germans to make them impassable.

That was where Buck Dickson, his men, and their bags full of maps and top secret orders entered the picture. Contrary to what the Pathfinders might have jokingly asserted, the S-2s hadn't only piggybacked Lieutenant Crouch's transport to stoke their curiosity. Their top secret mission was to reconnoiter the gun emplacements in Saint-Martin-de-Varreville, as well as an artillery garrison billeted in the nearby hamlet of Mézières, where the Germans had appropriated a cluster of eleven farmhouses, barns, and stables for their use. Coded W-X-Y-Z by G2 Intelligence, the complex had been bombed twice in a week, the first time by the RAF in late May, then again earlier that night by B-26 Marauders from the U.S. Air Force's 394th Bombardment Group, stationed at the RAF airfield at Boreham, Essex. But the chiefs in no way trusted the job to airpower alone. Dickson had been ordered to assess the strength of the enemy forces there and determine an overland route that the 502nd Infantry's 2nd Battalion could use to attack and destroy the gun emplacements.

But things did not at all go as planned for his team. As the last three men to exit Plane 1, they were seriously affected by the delay caused by Mangoni's stumble and did not clear the door until Crouch had doubled back over the peninsula and sped up for his trip home. Consequently, they'd landed far from Lillyman and the other paratroopers without having the slightest idea where they were relative to their location . . . and, more critically, to the position of the gun batteries they were supposed to scout out.

Dickson's jump itself went smoothly, and for that he was thankful. He'd barely had time to feel himself falling through the air when he came down in tall grass, moonlight pouring over him from the cloudless sky, washing over the grass so it almost looked like a carpet of silver tinsel. The night was silent around him—almost eerily so. He could hear nothing but his own anxious breath.

Still gathering his wits, he had some trouble escaping his parachute harness and set his M3 submachine gun down on the ground while working free of it. When he finally got that accomplished, he collected and repacked his gear and started to move off to find his men.

The lieutenant had gone about a dozen yards when he froze in his tracks, as if struck by cold lightning. He'd left the grease gun somewhere behind him in the field.

With a quick about-face, Dickson scrambled back to the spot where he'd dropped from the sky—or what he thought was the same spot. The grass was everywhere around him, coming up to his knees, one area resembling the next in the darkness. Cursing his stupidity, he squatted down on all fours and desperately felt around for the weapon, patting the ground, groping for it at the bottom of the high, flowing blades of grass.

The lieutenant expelled a long sigh of relief when his hands finally touched the grease gun's cool metal barrel. He didn't know what had guided them to it in the darkness, and didn't much care. The main thing was he'd found the weapon. Any fool knew you couldn't fight a war without a gun.

Standing up out of the grass like a surfacing diver, Dickson shouldered the weapon and got back to looking for his men. The countryside was quiet around him; he heard nothing but the night sounds one might have expected in any meadow anywhere: insects humming and chirruping, owls hooting, frogs croaking, and over and around it all the whisper of the breeze as it shifted through the field. He could have been in Kansas, Nebraska, or even Western Maryland, where he'd attended college . . . except that the hedgerows growing on all sides were undeniable reminders of how far he was from those places.

Alone and disoriented, Dickson moved off along the troop carrier's line of flight. For him, the silence had an almost perilous quality, leading his mind in unwanted and unsettling directions. What if the weather had taken a bad turn after the Pathfinder flights left England, forcing the invasion to be postponed again? If there hadn't been enough time to recall the troopers before they'd jumped? It didn't seem a likely scenario, but *what if*? The men who'd been flown here aboard the transport would be left to fend for themselves. To survive in enemy territory, possibly for several weeks, with only the supplies, ammunition, and meager chocolate D rations they carried on their backs.

Gnawed by uncertainty, Dickson went off seeking Ott and Clark. Fortunately they'd landed in nearby fields, and he was soon able to locate them, aided by the clicking of their signal bugs and the plentiful moonlight. But in spite of his relief at finding the S-2s, he knew the clock was running down on the arrival of the 2nd Battalion. They would have no time for a breather.

Kneeling low in the grass, the intelligence men spread their maps across their knees and studied them carefully by the light of their flashlights.

That was when the loud, rumbling thunder of antiaircraft fire shook the night.

Dickson looked up into the sky. *So much for the invasion being on hold.* Tracers had lit up the western horizon, a brilliant, pulsing glare that left all three men momentarily overwhelmed. But within seconds the rapt, fascinated expressions on their faces would be replaced with naked horror. A stricken C-47 transport had appeared above them, gushing flames, streaking down to earth like a meteor. If there were men aboard, they would be doomed.

Stunned, Dickson realized almost an hour had passed since his jump. The sheer volume of gunfire left him with no doubt that the main wave of airborne troops had arrived and met heavy resistance from German shore defenses. He also acknowledged, with a sinking feeling in his gut, that it was much too late to reconnoiter the battery at Saint-Martin-de-Varreville before the paratroops of the 2nd Battalion hit the ground.

Still, he'd learned to stick with the drill back in Western MD's ROTC program, and it all started with following orders. Unless those orders changed, they would bear toward their objective. There might yet be useful intelligence that his team could relay to headquarters about the gun emplacements.

Their purpose set, they folded away their maps and moved northward in the quaking, battle-torn night.

17.

Minutes earlier to the northwest, Frank Lillyman and his Pathfinders had started deploying their markers. Having stealthily
crossed one field after another, slipping between hedgerows with
Wilhelm and Williams leading the way, they'd found a suitable
pasture behind the Saint-Germain church. Jones had virtually carried Smith, who could hardly walk at all and was doing his best
not to slow the team up.

Lillyman knew they were still about a mile south of their original target area. But he'd taken into account that one man was hob-
bled, and that carrying their heavy radar and signaling equipment
over enemy-controlled terrain would be difficult in the little time
they had left.

All things considered, this field was their best bet. It was slightly
larger than the others they'd passed through and had only a sparse,
scattered growth of trees—and the wider and clearer, the better for
descending paratroopers. With the Five-Oh-Deuce transports due
to come roaring in, he'd decided his team had gone far enough.

Quick to carry out his orders, Jones, Wilhelm, and a couple of
the others removed the battery-powered Holophane lights from their
cardboard boxes and laid them out in a precise T formation—three
panels for the horizontal top bar and four for the vertical leg, with

the leg pointed in the direction of the jump and the crossbar marking the arrival point. The transports were to fly straight up the leg to the crossbar, where the jumpmasters would give the go commands to the paratroopers.

Set twenty-five yards apart and mounted on extendible tripods, the Holophanes had bright frosted-glass panels on their upper surfaces and emitted a low-level radiance in the direction from which the C-47s would approach. By placing them on tripods, the Pathfinders meant for them to be easily seen from overhead while, in theory at least, remaining nearly invisible to German infantry patrols at ground level.

Lillyman's T was amber, the identifying color for Drop Zone A. The T panels meant for Drop Zone C, at Hiesville, were red; Drop Zone D, outside Sainte-Marie-du-Mont, was to have lit up green. As a redundant signal to the incoming pilots and navigators, the bottom panel, or tail, of the T was its Morse code light. Using a telegraph key connected to the tail with a cable about eight yards long, one of the men would repeatedly blink the sequence for the letter A—a dot and a dash—so there would be no chance of a plane mistaking one DZ for another if there was some unforeseen snafu with the color panels, or in the event they were blown out by enemy fire.

The operation wasn't complicated, but it required Jones and his fellow signalmen to be proficient at using a new technology—or a new adaptation of technology—and to have the wits to work coolly and swiftly under tense conditions. All their long weeks at Pathfinder school in North Witham, all their arduous training jumps and rehearsals, had been designed to prepare them for a task that could take no more than ten minutes to execute from start to finish.

The same concentrated time frame applied to assembling the Eureka equipment. Lillyman had ordered Council and Walton to mount the unit in a treetop, and they'd shimmied up its trunk as Zamanakos kept lookout on the ground. The cue for triggering the Holophanes would be the sound of the approaching transports: when the signalmen heard their engines rumbling over the horizon, they would turn them on, one operator to a panel, and then hurry out of the sudden glare to avoid enemy eyes while remaining close enough to guard them against attack. It was the responsibility of the man with the telegraph key to stay in position even under fire.

At first, things went without a hitch for both Lillyman's T/3s and signal operators. But that was to change in a flash—literally.

With the T laid into position, Wilhelm's fingers were too fast for his own good again, finding the light switch well before the transports were in earshot. He barely had time to realize what he'd done when the Holophane beamed up into the sky like a searchlight, its brightness outlining the surprised troopers near the T in stark silhouette.

Horrified and furious at himself, Wilhelm was fumbling to turn the light back off when a series of machine-gun volleys rattled from the hedgerows. Then he heard the *whump* of mortar rounds detonating in the open field nearby.

We've had it, he told himself, swearing under his breath. How could he have done something like this again?

Rocca, standing with him, was equally dismayed. It sounded as if half the German Army had opened up on them.

Under increasing fire now, the signalmen stayed put near the valuable Holophanes. Their job was to do whatever they could to prevent them from being shot out. Council and Walters, meanwhile, clung to their treetop perches with the radar transmitter, using the bushy foliage for concealment.

The machine guns kept discharging from the bushes. With his eyes focused on their muzzle flash, Lillyman weighed his orders to avoid engaging the enemy and decided he had no recourse but to make an exception. He waved two of the Pathfinders toward the hedgerow, adding, with characteristic bravado, a few words about "teaching those Krauts the error of their ways." Then he watched the pair of troopers dash into the shadows, staying back to guard the T with the rest of his men.

The German machine-gun nest had been dug into the ground deep in the bordering thicket. Getting as close as they dared, the troopers pulled the pins on a couple of grenades and lobbed them in its direction.

Yards away, Lillyman heard the loud *whumph* of the detonations . . . and then the volleys stopped. Everything was suddenly quiet. He waited until he saw his men returning and then exhaled.

But his mission was far from accomplished, and he could only hope the Germans didn't send out reinforcements. At this point, there was little or nothing his Pathfinders could do but await the coming of the planes.

Lillyman would remember that wait as the longest of his entire life.

18.

Captain Basil Jones had gotten a flash of inspiration.

His orders from the admiralty were to stay on patrol against German warships, to stop for nothing that didn't represent a direct threat to the Allied invasion force. As an officer of the Royal Navy and commander of the 10th Flotilla, he was bound by his fidelity to duty and did not intend to disobey those commands.

Neither was it Jones's intention, however, to leave American paratroopers and airmen floundering in the Channel. There was, to be sure, a chance they were German spies. But if they were who and what they claimed to be—and his eyes, brain, and intuition told him they were—the skipper knew that by ignoring the men he would likely sentence them to death.

Stop or don't.

His choices were mutually exclusive, out-and-out contradictions . . . or were they?

Making his decision, Jones ordered his steersmen to circle the evacuees at slow speed and prepare to drop the lifeboats. He would save as many of them as he could without stopping the ship. As long as it kept moving, he could honestly say it had remained on uninterrupted patrol, and no one could claim he was at all violating his orders.

HMS *Tartar* wound her way around the struggling men, following their "ahoys" and other calls for help, picking them out of the water one, two, or three at a time. Overseeing the rescue effort, Jones found himself face-to-face with one dripping wet trooper whose features were still blackened with camo grease. Shivering, soggy, water pooling around his jump boots, he stood on deck and took a wary assessment of his surroundings.

"Who the hell's navy is this anyway?" he grunted truculently.

The skipper just grinned at him. Whatever slender doubts he'd had about these men being bona fide Americans had been dispelled once the paratrooper asked his question. It was an introduction he would never forget.

The rescue effort went on for about half an hour. Somehow, every last airman and paratrooper from the downed transport was brought safely aboard the destroyer. Most were nicked up, but none too badly hurt. Wheeler, the man Sergeant Malley had accidentally cut with his pocketknife, was the most seriously injured among the group, and Jones had him rushed to the infirmary for medical treatment. The rest were given an immediate taste of English hospitality: warm showers, fresh dry British uniforms, and shots of hot buttered rum—or grog, as their hosts called it—to take the chill out of their bones.

The group's participation in the D-Day invasion had ended. For some of them, especially Richard Wright, it was a profound letdown. He'd wanted to be in the vanguard of the fight against Nazi evil, to go to war alongside his friend Salty Harris, and had never gotten his chance that night. But he'd promised himself he would make up for it, and it was a pledge he took very seriously.

Within a few days, Wright and the others in his unit were turned over to the Air/Sea Rescue Services, brought back to England, and held behind bars for seventy-two hours while their status as American paratroopers was verified. More or less unscathed, their stick hadn't suffered a single loss in a calamity that could have easily taken every life aboard their flight.

Not all the Pathfinder teams would be so blessed.

19.

Along with the rest of his stick, Private Salty Harris came down almost on target at the outskirts of Hiesville.

The C-47 from which he'd jumped had carried one of five Pathfinder teams assigned to mark off the area designated Drop Zone C. Clyde Taylor's V serial—Planes 4, 5, and 6—had brought Pathfinders from the 101 Airborne's 501st and 506th PIRs to light the way for hundreds of main wave paratroopers slated to drop on the DZ around one o'clock in the morning. The other two teams, members of the 502nd PIR, flew aboard Planes 19 and 20, the last Pathfinder transports to leave North Windham airfield. Their mission was to guide in several hundred CG-4A Waco gliders from the 327th Glider Infantry Regiment by establishing illuminated runways in their landing zones. Towed across the Channel by C-47s, the wood, metal, and cloth gliders each carried a complement of thirteen troops and their equipment, including a Willys jeep and a howitzer or trailer.

From an operational standpoint there was little difference between preparing an area for paratroopers and preparing one for glider landings. Although larger and flatter than paratrooper drop zones, the glider LZs were still to be marked with Eureka beacons and lighted Ts. But the Pathfinders descending to mark their runways would run into much heavier resistance than Lillyman's group.

This was no coincidence. While Field Marshal Rommel had erroneously thought the main blow of the amphibious and naval assault would come farther east, he'd been correct in expecting gliders and paratroopers to descend on the peninsula. To prepare for an attack by airborne forces, he'd built up his defenses in many of their probable landing spots, flooding other areas to impede their movements.

Located near the strategically important Caen Canal, DZ C was a concentrated pocket of German ground troops and artillery, its perimeter bristling with rifle pits and machine-gun emplacements. The guns had been sending up steady streams of ammunition as Lieutenant Dwight Kroesch's Plane 5 made its pass, the flak so intense that Kroesch dropped shredded tinfoil as chaff to confuse enemy radar. Once the troopers jumped, he boomeranged back toward the coast for the return crossing to England at his top speed of 210mph, convinced he had a Luftwaffe night fighter on his tail.

The Pathfinders he'd dropped also ran into a firestorm—and had a longer than average descent in which to experience it. Kroesch had been among the transport pilots who opted to fly through the cloud bank rather than underneath it, seeking a hole from which he could see the ground. He'd found one at about eight hundred feet, four times the height at which Lieutenant Crouch had deployed his troopers. The extra time the men spent in the air gave the Germans a longer and better opportunity to shoot them out of it.

Salty Harris had been badgered by volleys throughout his drop and got no respite after making landfall. With ammunition spurting at him from the hedgerows, he tried to separate the oilskin bag containing his Eureka from his parachute harness, but it was all tangled up in the straps.

The guns kept firing away as he struggled to extricate the boxy unit, their salvos pulsing through the air around him. Desperate to escape the Germans' crosshairs, Harris finally ran for cover with the transmitter still strapped to his chest.

But not all the Pathfinders who came under immediate fire could run. Coming in on a separate flight, T/5 Richard Lisk bore one of his team's two Eurekas and was supposed to set it up for the gliders. An off-balance landing in a pasture left him with a fractured foot—and there was no medic nearby to give him a shot of morphine. As German bullets peppered the field, he stayed down on his belly, crawled to an open ditch alongside a hedgerow, and then tumbled down into it.

Several of Lisk's teammates would soon pass the spot where he'd hidden in the darkness, but aside from sharing some water out of their canteens, there was nothing they could do to help him. Unlike Snuffy Smith with Captain Lillyman's team, Lisk couldn't walk at all. His group had precious little time to find and mark the LZ and would have to leave him behind, promising to return when they'd completed their mission.

Burrowed down in the loamy soil, Lisk hid there in nervous silence as the troopers moved on toward their objective . . . but he wasn't alone for long. Within minutes, he heard the sound of heavy, booted footsteps approaching the ditch. Then low German voices.

Lisk held his breath, his body flat to the ground. The enemy foot patrol came close, closer, tramping past the ditch, kicking loose clods of soil into his face with the toes of their boots. He knew he'd be lucky to be taken prisoner if they discovered him— every member of the airborne was aware of Hitler's threat to have paratroopers shot as spies.

And that wasn't the only thing weighing on his mind.

He had the Eureka unit with him, a highly guarded piece of military technology. He couldn't let it fall into enemy hands. His orders were to activate the explosive charge inside it before that happened. To blow it to smithereens. But that wouldn't be possible with the Germans passing within an arm's reach.

Lisk knew that if he so much as twitched, they would see him. And if they saw him, they would never give him a chance to pull the det cord. He'd be captured or dead before he did it. The unit would fall into their hands. Even if they couldn't figure out how to replicate it, they might be able to learn the frequencies the Allies were using for their beacons.

His breath in his throat, his foot thudding with pain, Lisk watched and waited in the ditch, his only concealment the dark of night and the long moon shadows cast by the hedgerow behind him.

20.

About two miles south of DZ C, Drop Zone D was to be marked by a detachment of Pathfinders representing the 501st and 506th PIRs and occupying Planes 7, 8, and 9 of their serial.

The Three Kings were aboard Plane 8, and it was no accident that they had flown in the same stick.

T/5 Joseph Haller, Private David W. Hadley, and Private Lubimer Dejanovich had met back at Camp Mackall, South Carolina, in 1943, when they were teammates in the communications platoon of the 501 HQ's 1st Battalion. Hitting it off big, they had stuck together like glue before, during, and after drills. They'd also gotten on their company commander's nerves together, although for different reasons.

"We are the Three Kings . . . I am King ONE!" Haller had once stated.

The name stuck, although as far as the CO, Captain John Simmons, was concerned, he was nothing but a royal headache. Of Austrian descent, Haller had a booming voice to match his rowdy personality and could be happily obnoxious when he'd razz the guys in his outfit with his I'm-a-member of-the-Master-Race routine.

"Why am I always so *right*?" he would ask himself aloud in the barracks. His answer? "It must be my Aryan blood!"

While striking his best Nazi brownshirt pose, Haller also hammed it up by declaring he would someday rule the world, or by blurting out random German phrases just to aggravate people—and it worked, especially with an increasingly frustrated Simmons.

Dejanovich had followed Haller's lead by mining his Serbian origins for joke material. "Once we land in Europe, I'm going over the hill to join Tito!" he'd state, prompting the straitlaced Simmons to wonder if he was a Communist sympathizer.

It didn't help that Dejanovich, like Haller, would sometimes enjoy showing off that he was fluent in his ancestral tongue. Meanwhile, Hadley, a willing foil for his pals, got a kick out of their skewed senses of humor and didn't seem to mind getting lumped in as a troublemaker with them.

Simmons would eventually have his fill of all three. When the experimental Pathfinder units made a call for commo techs in the winter of '44, he strongly suggested that he wanted them to move on.

"We'd like to have you in the Pathfinders because you can speak German," he told Haller.

It was a lame explanation, but Haller took his hint with predictable bluster. "If it's my time to die, I'm going to die no matter where I am," he said, adding, "You want me in the Pathfinders, I'll join the Pathfinders."

To Simmons's great delight, Dejanovich and Hadley followed suit. The Three Kings were hastily shoved off to England, where they would train under Joel Crouch and Frank Lillyman at North Witham. Lieutenant Albert Watson, a mess officer with the battalion who'd also fallen into disfavor with Simmons, would be encouraged to go on his way with them.

As their senior commander, Watson would have doubtless had a major say in choosing Haller and crew for his stick on the night of the invasion, which may account for how they all wound up aboard the same transport.

True to form, Haller had managed to irritate his stick mates while crossing the Channel. He'd been drinking coffee nonstop at base to calm his nerves, and once in flight had needed to answer to his bladder for all the cups he'd consumed. Glancing toward the bathroom stall at the rear of the troop compartment, he decided he would never fit inside it with his equipment load, and instead went to the open jump door and relieved himself—not taking the backdraft into account.

If Haller had been the only one to wind up dripping with urine, the other troopers might have gotten a good laugh at his expense. But when the men closest to the door got it blown in their faces, they bombarded him with curses and insults.

Their aggravation notwithstanding, it wasn't long before everyone aboard the plane quieted down. Bound for Drop Zone D between the villages of Vierville and Angoville-Au-Plain, their serial started taking heavy flak as soon as it turned overland—and the machine-gun and antiaircraft fire would intensify as they neared the DZ. Here the German troops were even more prepared than those to the south at Drop Zone C, where the Pathfinders were already meeting with stiff resistance.

Its central area a flat, open pasture with a big farmhouse at one side, the DZ offered the paratroopers little cover as they descended, while providing the defenders with numerous convenient hiding places at the field's periphery. With flare guns to light the darkness and confuse the troopers, they had machine guns and mortars concealed in the hedgerows on three sides, aiming them into the pasture to cover the areas where the invaders would touch down.

The Germans would also benefit from an unhappy pair of delays that had beset the American transports en route.

The first hitch for their formation had been running into the belt of clouds along the coast. All three C-47s had gotten lost in the vaporous gray mist, missed their last turning point, and flown clear across the peninsula before their aircrews sighted the east coast below them.

Sweeping around in a wide circle, they had turned back toward the DZ from the southeast, only to meet with outbreaks of heavy flak as they sped overland to make their passes. The pilots had repeatedly jinked left and right to avoid incoming fire, contributing to the delay in their arrival at the drop zone. When they finally gave the Pathfinders the green light, it was 12:47 A.M., seventeen minutes later than planned, and thirty-five minutes after Lillyman and his men had made their landings to the north.

It was a critical lag. By this time German troops across the Cotentin had been roused from their barracks and frantically sent out to man their posts. At first none of the defenders, including Rommel himself—who had left the coast for Berlin to attend his wife Lucie's birthday party and was there when he received news of the airborne attack—suspected that the Allies had begun their invasion. Most believed they were fending off a limited commando strike. But despite their surprise and confusion, they were strongly entrenched throughout the peninsula and well primed to be "sitting at their arms" once the alarm got out.

The German defenders at Drop Zone D were among the best positioned in the early going. They opened fire on the Pathfinders from the hedgerows even as they made landfall, using flare pistols to light up the field around them, hitting them with a fusillade of machine-gun fire and mortar shells—and that wasn't the only punishing surprise in store for the invaders. After sloshing gasoline all over the farmhouse at the edge of the pasture, the Germans had stood ready to start it on fire as the C-47s arrived, meaning to blind their aircrews with the glare and immolate the troopers who might be unable to avoid plunging down on top of it.

With the Pathfinders' jump having occurred so late, there was only minutes between their arrival and the rumbling sound of the 506th PIR's main wave transports approaching in the western sky—the Germans' cue to put their torches to the farmhouse. It went up instantly, gripped by a giant orange claw of flame.

Although their planes had come in low, the troopers felt as if their descent took a hundred years. With the German guns turned skyward, bullets riddled some of the men's silk as they dropped into the swirling inferno of the field. Others were killed before their feet touched the earth, and still more were mowed down as they landed. Those who crashed into the trees at the fringes of the pasture had to cut themselves out of their harnesses under heavy fire. At least one jumper, Stanley Suwarsky, who'd leaped from Plane 6, was shot to death as he dangled helplessly from a bough. He would be the first American soldier to perish in the Normandy invasion.

In the middle of the field, the Pathfinders at first lay still to avoid the bullets and tracers sizzling through the tall grass around them. But they knew they could not stay out in the open, where they were easy targets. Within a few minutes they began inching toward the hedgerows amid the flames and machine-gun salvos, their chins down in the dirt, crawling on their stomachs to avoid crossfire over their heads. They had to find cover and set up their lights and beacons.

Amid the chaos of the landing, a group of them managed to collect themselves and sneak up on a couple of German machine-gun emplacements. Getting their grenades loose, they tossed them into the nests and hit the dirt. The explosions took out the enemy soldiers at their posts.

With those guns silenced, Lieutenant Watson got a needed opening to rally several of his men. Among them was Joe Haller, the self-anointed King One, who also held the distinction of being one of Watson's Eureka operators. The Germans spraying him with fire from several directions, Haller dragged his unit into the shrubbery, fully aware it could have slowed him down enough to get him killed.

Watson knew it would be impossible for his signalmen to lay out their T with machine-gun rounds and mortars coming at them from all sides. Moreover, the light from the blazing farmhouse across the field would be far brighter than the panels, rendering them almost useless to the pilots. The radar beacon was now Team D's best bet for guiding in the formation.

Haller rushed to set it up, getting the antenna out of the oil-skin's outside pocket, connecting it to the unit, and then telescoping it to its full eleven-foot height. The sound of the planes was so loud he could almost feel the vibration in his bones. They were close, almost on top of the field. But he could only hope there was still time for the lead plane's Rebecca to zone in on the radar beam.

Slipping on his headset, Haller powered up the Eureka, calibrated its dials to the designated signal frequency, and began transmitting.

Without lights to mark the drop zone, he used the device's added radio Morse code function to send out a dash and two dots for the letter D.

The planes appeared seemingly at once and began to release their sticks, the shadowy forms of the paratroopers dotting the night sky as they came down into the field.

Looking up from below, surrounded by the enemy, Watson, Haller, and the rest of the Pathfinders watched them descend in the glare of the fiercely burning farmhouse. Although hardly out of danger, they knew they were no longer on their own.

The Allied invasion of Normandy had begun.

CHAPTER TWO

1.

T/5 Maynard Beamesderfer remembered exactly when he'd started thinking it might be fun to jump out of an airplane with a parachute. He was sixteen or seventeen years old and on a family trip up to New York to see the '39 World's Fair.

The visit was something special for the Beamesderfers. Maynard's father was a farmhand in Lebanon, Pennsylvania, and there was never much spending money at home, and the teenager lived in a world with relatively narrow borders.

Life revolved around work for the males of the family, and he always did his part to add to the household income. In his final year of high school, Maynard—his friends just called him "Beamy"—had gotten a job at the Hershey chocolate plant about five miles from where he lived and had worked there four hours a day at thirty-five cents an hour, taking the nickel trolley over with some of his friends. During the harvest seasons, he'd earned extra wages picking tomatoes and tobacco and other crops at the local produce farms. It had helped that he spoke the broken German called Pennsylvania Dutch—his dad had been raised a Dunker, though he wasn't very religious—because that was all the old farmers knew, and they wouldn't hire anyone who couldn't communicate in the dialect.

It had taken the Beamesderfers a while to save up enough money for the World's Fair, and Beamy went with only a dollar to spend on the attractions. But the moment he set eyes on the Parachute Jump, he was hooked. The tower was a lofty two hundred fifty feet high, and for a quarter a ride, he was strapped into a seat and pulled up on cables to its summit, then dropped to the ground under one of the brightly colored parachutes.

Beamy had gotten on the Jump several times, waiting in the long lines and spending most of his dollar on it. The ride had electrified him and he wouldn't forget it. He'd thought it was just plain great.

It was about a year later that he'd seen a U.S. Army recruitment film for airborne troopers. This was right after Pearl Harbor, at a movie matinee back home in Lebanon. He had never heard of soldiers that jumped into battle with parachutes, and had figured it must be something new for the service. In the reel, the troopers wore soft leather frap hats, and the narrator explained that the drop towers they used for their drills had come from the World's Fair. That made Beamy remember his thrilling experience on the rides.

The jump training sounded like a "real good deal." Being a country boy, working on the farms, he'd had dreams of seeing the bigger world around him. Whenever he and his classmates had traveled to Philly for the state basketball tournaments, the boys there had harassed them with calls of *"Here come the shitkickers!"* and Beamy had hardly blamed them. His school didn't even have a hardwood court, and he played basketball outdoors on the dirt. Beamy and his teammates were very proud they could compete at all with the boys at the city armory.

With the draft having begun in 1940, Beamy's parents and relatives had braced for the inevitability that he'd be pulled into the service at some point—of the dozen boys in his high school class, only the three strict Mennonites had legal exemptions. But his family still reacted with surprise when he told them he planned to leave school and enlist at eighteen, with a year left before graduation. The family members on his father's side were especially taken aback. As Dunkers, they were religious pacifists. He would be the first of their clan ever to join the armed forces.

But Beamy had never taken to schoolwork. Though his teachers all agreed he was a bright kid, he had a lot of energy he couldn't seem to channel in positive directions and had gotten into hot water so often that his sister's friends called him the devil of the neighborhood. In their hearts, the Beamesderfers may have felt the army was the best thing for his future.

Beamy would practically go straight from the recruitment office in Pennsylvania to Fort Benning, Georgia, where the rookies trained for a couple of months before they did some jumping at the drop zones across the Chattahoochee River in Alabama. The drills had been strenuous, and the NCOs hard as nails, but he'd made it through, and found the night jumps easy and fun. The Alabama DZs had been fairly well cleared of trees, fences, and other jump hazards, so you didn't have to worry about hitting much except watermelon fields, and hardly any of the men thought landing in one of them was too awful.

After another two months or so, Beamy had been assigned to the 101st Airborne's 501st Parachute Infantry at Fort Bragg, North Carolina. There at the 62,000-acre Camp Mackall training facility, things had gotten harder. Mackall was a rough-up place. When you were there, you got the sense you were getting ready for something that wouldn't be too pleasant.

That feeling would grow among the paratroopers in the spring of 1943, once they were sent to participate in combined, large-scale tank and infantry maneuvers with Patton's Third Army in Tennessee. There they would drop into swampy areas and be given realistic mission objectives, and everybody agreed the jumps weren't fun anymore. For Beamy and the other trainees they were becoming scary and pressurized. With each successive exercise you'd carry a heavier load of equipment, and if you didn't successfully complete your mock operations, or handle your chute and gear with precision, you'd be reprimanded. Beamy caught hell plenty of times for things like not folding his chute to specifications or failing to leave it at a prearranged pickup spot . . . but it wasn't just that. The geography in Tennessee was similar to Western Europe, and the lifelike maneuvers told him the war was getting closer.

The Screaming Eagles had impressed the brass with their performance in the Tennessee war games, and in January of 1944 the entire division was transferred overseas to Berkshire, England. The exercises that took place there over the next several months, BEAVER, TIGER, and EAGLE, were the most rigorous the 101st had yet undergone. Assigned to capture roads and bridges from simulated beaches, the men all realized these maneuvers were dress rehearsals for the invasion of Europe and conducted them with a heightened sense of gravity. Now the war wasn't just close. It was breathing down their necks.

Beamy's introduction to the Pathfinders began one day early in '44. He'd gone off base for lunch with an uncle who lived in the United Kingdom, and they were at a table speaking Pennsylvania Dutch when an officer seated behind them overheard some of their conversation.

The brass hat waited until they'd finished their meal and then came around to talk. "Are you Mr. Beamesderfer?" he asked.

Beamy told him he was.

"I want you to report to HQ," he said flatly.

Beamy had sat looking at the officer with apprehension. He didn't recognize him and was wondering if he'd done something wrong. It wouldn't have been his first go-round with military discipline—he'd had an episode or three in the village while on weekend pass and gone AWOL a few times, that sort of thing. But he couldn't think of any recent infractions that could have gotten him in hot water.

At headquarters, Beamesderfer was informed about the new volunteer Pathfinder unit and told their job would be to land behind the lines ahead of other paratroopers and set up special homing devices. Like Joe Haller, he learned that his name had already been submitted for consideration and was given the rigmarole about it being because of his familiarity with the German language and how that would be an asset behind the lines.

Beamesderfer had accepted the explanation as truthful, or at least kept it to himself if he ever suspected he'd simply gotten on his commanding officer's bad side. Whatever he may have thought privately about why he was called in, he'd agreed to the assignment. Soon he was at North Witham taking the special training under the auspices of the IX TCC, sequestered behind its fencing and gates, doing the night jumps, and learning how to operate the navigational equipment in preparation for the invasion.

Tonight it had all become real. After months of training and preparation, the war was finally upon him. His team of Pathfinders had left the airdrome on Plane 20, bound for Drop Zone C to ready the overlapping landing zone for the Waco glider lifts—designated Drop Zone E. The first of the lifts was scheduled to arrive at four in the morning, the second in the early evening on D-Day.

Their flight across the Channel hadn't been too bad given the full range of nerve-wracking possibilities. The shaking and swaying of the transport had made some of the troopers lower their heads between their knees, and the puddles they left on the floor weren't exactly pleasing to the nose. But the transport hadn't taken any antiaircraft fire for most of the trip, and that was something they appreciated to a man. Beamy supposed the worst part of it for them was the lingering element of uncertainty over what they were getting into. They knew they were supposed to set up the beacons for the gliders, help the 3rd Battalion troops dropping nearby clear obstacles to the landings, and then join the rest of the 501st PIR in capturing the Douve River lock at La Barquette.

But many couldn't shake the same uninvited doubts that had beset Lieutenant Buck Dickson in Plane Number 1. They wondered what would happen if they couldn't make contact with the arriving troops—or if the invasion was delayed again for some reason and no one showed up. The closer they got to France, the more these thoughts gnawed at their minds.

As the transport had made its left turn over the Cotentin Peninsula, the tension in the troop compartment became palpable. German flak guns opened up in force, almost as if making up for lost time. Beamesderfer found himself glad he'd remembered one particular item of equipment that hadn't been issued by the quartermaster—a pocket copy of the New Testament that his mother had told him to carry. There had been no small amount of friction between his parents throughout their marriage, mostly due to her strict religious beliefs clashing with his father's indifference. Though Beamy guessed his own religiosity fell somewhere in the middle, he felt keeping that little book close, and seeking guidance from above, would help him get through the dangerous times ahead.

He was very aware of having it with him when Lieutenant Henley, his stick leader, gave the go command. Moving to the door, his stomach full of butterflies, he looked down at a field that was dotted with orange flames. Though the men couldn't have known it, they had slightly missed their mark at DZ C and were about to be dropped closer to Drop Zone D, where the Germans had laid their fiery trap for the paratroops and gliders.

At twenty-seven minutes past midnight, the Pathfinders aboard Plane 20 jumped into the mouth of hell.

2.

In Saint-Germain-de-Varreville to the south, Captain Lillyman had sent Wilhelm and Williams to recon the area around the field. He was convinced the machine gunners who'd been harrying them would not have set up their post in isolation. There had to be some place nearby they were using as a de facto command center.

The scouts returned with word that they'd seen a farmhouse at the edge of the pasture with a Nazi infantry vehicle outside it. That confirmed Lillyman's suspicions. The single car told him they likely wouldn't find too many Germans there, but it only took one to sound an alert about American soldiers nearby.

Wanting a closer look, he decided to head over to the house with the scouts.

When he and his men reached the farmhouse, they saw a civilian in the doorway, calmly smoking a pipe as if he'd been expecting them. "*Bosche*," he said, and jerked a thumb back over his shoulder at the stairs.

Lillyman recognized the derogatory French slang word for their occupiers; loosely translated it meant something like "pig head."

Racing up to the second story, the paratroopers found the enemy soldier asleep in bed wearing crisp white pajamas, his officer's uniform folded away, a bottle of champagne at the bedside.

He'd obviously had no problem getting comfortable in a home where he was an unwanted guest.

A single crack of a rifle echoed down from the little room. When the three Americans emerged and hurried back downstairs, they were carrying the champagne bottle with them. They had dispatched the German officer and, as Lillyman would later put it, "expropriated" the bubbly.

Whatever term he favored, the satisfied Frenchman puffing tobacco in the front door didn't seem to mind them taking it one bit.

3.

Back in the field, Captain Lillyman looked up and saw the sky filled with the billowing chutes of American paratroopers, hundreds of them afloat in the darkness like jellyfish descending through the sea. As Zamanakos would recall, the planes had seemed to "come in from all points of the compass." The cloud bank that had created so much confusion for Crouch's pilots was now causing the main body of airborne infantrymen to jump wide of their marks.

But the transports had arrived, and their pilots used the beacons to stay reasonably close to the overall Allied objectives. Lillyman took that as a qualified success.

These lights never looked so bright in training, he thought. That night they seemed like searchlights, leading him to half expect they would draw the enemy to his position. But the only German soldiers he'd seen since leaving the farmhouse had been in a bicycle patrol, and they'd quickly pedaled off as if wanting no part of the troopers.

It was now past midnight. Alone and in small groups, jumpers from various units straggled toward the DZ after making landfall. As they began to arrive, Lillyman sent out word for all the Pathfinders in his serial to gather at the little church, where they were to drop off their lights and radar beacons and await further orders from their company commanders.

Meanwhile, two hundred yards to the east, Lieutenant Colonel Patrick Cassidy of the 502nd PIR's 1st Battalion had leaped from the forward plane of his V serial into streams of machine-gun fire that seemed to be aimed right at him. The guns tracked the men of this stick three-quarters of their way down to the ground and then angled up toward the aircraft overhead. As he plunged earthward, Cassidy was sure he would have been picked out of the air if their fire hadn't been redirected at the planes.

Suddenly he saw a paved road below—actually the juncture of two roads. His boots hit the macadam at the intersection, the impact sending a jolt up his spine. At the same time, his entire body was wrenched upward from the shoulders, as if by an impossibly huge rubber band. He fell to the pavement, realizing his parachute had gotten snagged on a low-hanging branch.

He was struggling to free himself from the chute when a machine gun began pouring rounds at him from the hedgerow across the road. Flat against the pavement, he reached for a grenade and prepared to hurl it toward the source of the fire.

Just then he heard planes flying overhead. Another group of transports had come in. The aircraft once again drew off the guns, buying him the seconds he desperately needed to wriggle out of his harness, orient himself east to west, and start crawling back along the line of flight. But he'd only gone a short distance when the fusillade resumed, bullets chewing up road around him.

He flattened again. A new group of C-47s passed overhead, dropping its paratroopers a short distance to the west. As the machine gun rattled up at the aircraft, Cassidy continued to move toward the alighting troopers, staying off the middle of the road, stitching out an evasive path between the hedges and ditches at its margins.

Then he heard a sound in the crossroads behind him—one that seemed jarringly out of context in his present surroundings. But there was no mistaking it for anything other than what it was:

Hoofbeats. *Galloping* hooves.

Cassidy shot a quick glance backward and saw the spectral form of a man on horseback plunging across the intersection, the horse's mane whipping over the sides of its long, muscular neck. He stared with nervous surprise as rider and mount vanished through a gap in the hedgerows, the drumming of hooves rapidly fading into the night. He didn't pause to wonder if the horseman was German or French, would not let his mind deviate from the goal of uniting with the other paratroopers. He had to keep moving.

He'd scurried a little farther along when he heard an artillery shell launch from behind the hedges. Diving to his belly, he felt the ground shudder beneath him as the mortar round detonated nearby with a crash, chunks of pavement flying in all directions. It was almost as if he were traversing an endless obstacle course, with every danger imaginable coming at him.

He waited. A second mortar round *whumped* down to the ground several feet away. There was a third, a fourth. Then the next serial of planes flew overhead, leading to another break in the fire. He pushed up off the road and sprinted forward.

About a hundred yards from where he'd started out, Colonel Cassidy heard a rustling noise on the other side of the hedges. It grew softer and more distant as he listened.

Scrambling up the dirt embankment, he found an opening where he could see through into the adjacent field.

Two men were moving away from him, walking briskly along the hedge toward the crossroads. With their backs turned, they were nothing more than shadows in the gloom.

Cassidy got his clicker from where it hung around his neck and snapped it. They kept walking without response. Had they failed to recognize the signal and mistaken it for the sound of an insect, indicating they were likely enemy soldiers? Or could they be Americans who'd just failed to hear it?

He'd no sooner asked himself these questions than somebody *did* respond—but it wasn't one of the pair he'd spotted.

Click-clack, click-clack!

Squinting into the darkness, Cassidy saw a third man trailing behind the others, much closer to where he was hunkered on the embankment. Although the colonel didn't recognize him at all, he immediately identified his American paratrooper's uniform.

"Where are you going?" Cassidy asked from his side of the hedgerow.

"We're looking for the colonel," the trooper replied.

Cassidy smiled thinly and told him they'd found their man. Pushing through the hedges, he realized he knew the soldiers who'd been walking with their backs to him. Both were staffers—his radioman, T/3 Leo Bogus, and his runner, Private Talmage New. The trooper who'd heard his click was a stranger who'd stumbled on the others while trying to locate his own platoon.

Colonel Cassidy would now lead the group toward the paratroopers he'd seen drop out of the sky, rallying men from his 1st Battalion along with misdropped soldiers belonging to other units. Crossing into another field, they found Lieutenant Colonel Robert Strayer, commander of the 506's 2nd Battalion, and his own mixed band of troopers. After a panel split in his chute, Strayer had landed hard, hurting his ankles and right knee. Although hardly able to walk, he joined Cassidy in moving through the hedgerows, assembling men from different sticks and looking for road signs that could help orient them. They soon came upon three of his officers, who'd pulled together still more strays and were gathering up supply bundles dropped from the transports. One of the officers, Captain Fred Hancock, had noticed a sign for the village of Foucarville about a mile and a half to their north. Checking his aerial map, Cassidy realized it would be a straight shot in the opposite direction to Objective W-X-Y-Z at Saint-Martin-de-Varreville—the same encampment Buck Dickson had been sent to reconnoiter for Strayer's 2nd Battalion.

But Captain Dickson and his men hadn't yet reported in. Nor had anyone from headquarters been able to raise them in the field. With their status and whereabouts unknown, Strayer and Cassidy had been left without close-up intelligence about the complex.

The lack of scouting information troubled Strayer. It was his job to destroy the big artillery guns at Saint-Martin-de-Varreville, while Cassidy's battalion cleaned out the German garrison three hundred yards to the west. Cassidy was then supposed to establish roadblocks at two key road crossings from Utah beach that ran past W-X-Y-Z—Exits 3 and 4—allowing the troops that were coming ashore to advance without opposition from German reinforcements.

For Strayer, his lack of a full complement of troopers for the mission was a major complication. The fact that the bulk of his men still hadn't assembled convinced him a large number had come down far outside their designated area and would need more time to reach it. He'd also found it increasingly laborious to get around on his bad leg and felt that would make him a sure drag on any force he might try to lead against the Germans at W-X-Y-Z.

That left the two colonels to decide how to proceed—and they immediately found themselves at odds. Strayer insisted on waiting for more of his troopers before heading toward the complex and refused to budge until they showed up. Sharply differing with him, Cassidy made it clear he intended to take his men and shove off with all due haste. He hadn't survived barrages of machine-gun fire and mortar shells only to risk leaving the gun battery in enemy hands and the road exits vulnerable to attack.

"I'll get going," he said. "We're ready."

Strayer wasn't swayed. He would stay back to gather his battalion and hopefully get hold of a vehicle to convey him to their objective. Since the gliders were coming in with jeeps aboard them, he was optimistic that wouldn't take long.

Their discussion was over. Cassidy's 1st Battalion and the stragglers who'd joined them would now spearhead the attack on the gun battery. As dawn crept up the eastern sky, they formed into a column and set out northward to Saint-Martin-de-Varreville, marching over the road instead of using the cover of the fields and bocage where the going would be safer but slower.

Cassidy was about halfway to his destination when he fortuitously crossed paths with Frank Lillyman and some of his Pathfinders. Though their meeting was unplanned, he'd find out they had important information to share with him.

4.

The hours after midnight had been busy ones for Lillyman. By two or three o'clock in the morning, the main body of paratroopers had been delivered by their transports, freeing him to venture from the drop zone in support of the 502's primary objective—the taking of the gun battery west of Utah Beach. Leaving a small detail with the Holophanes and injured troopers at the Saint-Germain church, he'd led a scouting party comprised of Wilhelm, Jones, and several others up and down the road toward Saint-Martin-de-Varreville, probing for enemy soldiers at its edges and wanting to learn what he could about the disposition of the German artillery that Lieutenant Dickson's still-missing team had been sent to recon.

A short while before running into Cassidy, Lillyman's party had gone as far south as the two exits near the W-X-Y-Z complex, traipsed off the road, and abruptly realized they were in the very spot where the gun emplacements were shown on their maps.

Surprise had flickered in their eyes. The site was a silent ruin, its soil pitted and blackened, torn up by the five-hundred-pound demolition bombs dropped in the two preparatory Allied airstrikes. Wherever they turned, the Pathfinders saw crates of German arms and supplies scattered about like scale-model pieces thrown from a violently upended tabletop—some with their lids still on, others blown to splintery bits, their disgorged contents randomly strewn around them.

There was no sign of the German troops that had occupied the site—only the weapons and equipment they'd left behind. A Renault R35 light tank seized from the French Army lay flipped over on its dome. Three of the four guns were gone, removed from their concrete bunkers. The remaining cannon, a 122mm Soviet howitzer captured on the Eastern Front, had been partly rolled out of the bunker that housed it when the structure collapsed into heaps of rubble, burying the portion of the weapon that was still inside. On inspection, Lillyman had concluded that the German artillerymen tasked with rescuing the cannon must have fled as the bombers made their run . . . and that the bunker had taken a direct hit.

And that was it. There was nothing else. The field was spooky and deserted.

Lillyman hadn't wanted to linger amid the debris. The emplacement had been a source of much nervous hand-wringing for U.S. Army brass, who would be landing more than twenty thousand troops at Utah beach in a scant few hours. He was eager to pass on word of his discovery.

After ordering a few of the men to stay behind at the abandoned gun position, he and Wilhelm had headed back up toward

Saint-Germain, where he'd planned to radio word of his find to his commanders from the church.

As it turned out that wouldn't be needed. Now several hundred men strong and made up of paratroopers from both the 101st and 82nd Airborne Divisions, Pat Cassidy's patchwork fighting force had appeared on the road ahead of Lillyman. Marching toward him in the predawn grayness, the dark-haired, smartly mustached colonel headed up the column.

Lillyman hastily told Cassidy what he'd seen up the road.

"I've got news for you," he said. "I scouted that coastal battery. It's thoroughly bombed out. No need to worry about that one."

The perceptible sigh of relief that escaped the colonel's lips would be shared by the entire U.S. 4th Infantry divisional command. A major obstacle to the landing had been neutralized.

Neither man was about to bask in his good fortune, though. Cassidy had yet to secure the beach exits for the infantry, and there was no telling what sort of resistance he'd encounter at the W-X-Y-Z barracks.

In a hurry to move on, the colonel ordered Lillyman to gather the rest of his men and head up to Foucarville, where he wanted to establish roadblocks to seal off the northern margin of his operational area, preventing German reinforcements from pushing down the road into it.

Lillyman snapped him a salute, wished him luck, and started toward his assigned destination. But within hours his group of Pathfinders would be given a new set of orders.

5.

Beamy Beamesderfer had landed in darkness and water up to his ankles.

During their four-year occupation of France, the Germans had regularly opened the Douve and Merderet River locks along a twelve-square-mile floodplain spreading out behind the Normandy coast and spanned by a small number of roads and bridges running inland from the beaches. The periodic floodings were likely trial runs for a possible Allied assault. If Rommel's forces could hold the bridges, and control the flow of the river and its offshoot canals, they would be able to bog down American and British tanks, gliders, and infantry in the marshes while ensuring their own troops had unimpeded access to the area. In that way, they could form a choking noose around the invaders.

The marsh into which Beamesderfer parachuted was less than six inches deep, but could precipitously drop to depths of six or eight feet in any of the countless irrigation ditches crisscrossing the field. The Cotentin's farmers had dug the ditches between seventy-five and a hundred yards apart, inadvertently laying the groundwork for these watery obstacle courses. A paratrooper might be wading ankle-deep across the marshland, step into one of the flooded pits, and suddenly find himself trying to swim in water over his head, weighted down by hundreds of pounds of equipment. Or he might plunge down into it and drown when making landfall. Situations of this type would bedevil the paratroopers who came down in Drop Zones C and D, killing scores of them before they ever saw a German soldier.

After he'd splashed into the marsh, Beamy had disentangled himself from his parachute and harness, let them drift off in the muck, and then gotten down flat on his stomach . . . or as flat as his chest and belly packs would allow. He'd been cold, uncomfortable, and scared. Dropping into the swamped fields was a nightmarish experience for the Pathfinders—especially so at the fringes of DZ D, near the village of Saint-Come-Du-Mont, where the enemy had taken hidden positions around the farmhouse.

Now Beamesderfer lay there in the muddy water as the flares and tracers scratched the darkness over his head. His combat uniform, woolen long johns, and boots were sopping wet, adding several pounds of weight to his equipment load. Water sloshing around his chin, he looked from side to side, discerned several figures moving about the field, and then heard them snap their clickers. They were almost certainly fellow Pathfinders, but with the darkness and blinding glare of the incendiaries playing havoc with his vision, it was hard to be sure they were members of his stick— and he was reluctant to raise his head for a better look. With machine guns chattering from the hedges, and tracer rounds zipping through the half-submerged grass like glowy snakes, he knew the LZ was hemmed in by Germans and that they could easily pick off him and the rest of the Pathfinders.

He also knew his group could not set out the light panels and radar transmitters in water and would have to seek out higher ground after they managed to assemble. In the meantime, they could only wait until the main wave flights arrived. If they couldn't depend on the troops that were coming in to rout the enemy from the hedges, their chances of success—and survival—would be close to zero.

The German fire got worse as the minutes wore on. Beamesderfer saw men around him drop into the marsh after being struck by bullets, heard the moans of the wounded in the darkness, and wondered if he would be next. He'd thought the sound of the transports flying in over the coast would be a relief, but the nightmare only worsened when the Germans put their torches to the farmhouse and it roared into flame like a colossal pyre.

Beamy lay there, wet, cold, and terrified. He felt no shame admitting later on that he lost control of his bowels. Remembering the Bible his mother had given him, he put his hand where he could feel its outline pressing against the outer fabric of his pocket, and prayed for a higher power to see him through. That helped him reach an inner place of calm, one to which he would return time and again when everything around him seemed almost too fearsome to bear.

When the first men of 3rd Battalion finally started coming in— some landing around him, others splashing over from adjacent fields—their guns and bazookas created sufficient cover for troopers from the two planeloads of Team E Pathfinders to reach a dry spot for their glider runway. Though Beamesderfer's stick had been decimated on landing—of the group who'd flown aboard Plane 20, eight were killed during or shortly after the jump—the assignment would be completed by the Five-Oh-Deuce team that jumped from Plane 19, the same transport that had carried Richard Lisk, the injured Eureka operator.

Plagued by mortars and enemy fire, Beamesderfer's team was nevertheless able to establish their lights and turn on their Eurekas by ten minutes to four in the morning. At four o'clock sharp, the transmitters made contact with their companion Rebecca units aboard the glider tows, and Colonel Mike Murphy, the pilot of the lead CG-4A Waco in the airlift dubbed the Chicago mission, began his descent upon the illuminated runway.

Beamesderfer, meanwhile, had gone off in search of his missing teammates. Unaware that most had been killed, he hoped they might have gone on toward the main regimental objective, the Douve River's La Barquette lock. He himself knew little about why the lock had been targeted. But the thought at Headquarters was to turn the Germans' own strategy of flooding the marshes against them. It was believed that if the airborne could seize the lock intact and hold it against all counterattack by the enemy, the marshes could be turned into a lake, imposing an extra barrier between the Germans and the Allies. Or they could "sit on" the lock and keep the marsh draining until they were ready to go forward.

As it turned out, Beamy would never reach La Barquette. In trying to find his regiment, he would tag up with a band of paratroopers headed southwest toward the Douve River, where their objective was to wire three bridges near the towns of Brevants and Carentan for demolition. Two were wooden footbridges they'd been instructed to blow with all due haste, and the third was a larger vehicular bridge the Allies hoped might be used by their own armor—if it could be captured and held. Otherwise it was also to be reduced to smoking rubble.

Like many of the groups wandering the peninsula that night, this one had been cobbled together from men belonging to different units. The 506th PIR demolition platoon assigned the mission had been widely scattered in the jump, and its leader was "picking up stragglers" to help him carry it out.

His name was Sergeant James Elbert "Jake" McNiece, and he was rapidly gaining a reputation as one of the toughest of the tougher-than-nails fighting men in the 101st Screaming Eagles.

6.

Some miles to the northeast of Drop Zones C and D, Lieutenant Buck Dickson was finding out the limitations of the M3 grease gun he'd almost left behind in the tall grass. It was a learning experience he hoped would not prove fatal.

He, Ott, and Clark had been wandering throughout the night, trying to figure out where they were and make their way to the Saint-Martin battery. In the course of roaming the fields, they'd found men from the 101st and the 82nd in similar predicaments and joined up with them as they sought their unit commands. Periodic brushes with German troops had eventually left the S-2s and a few others separated from the loosely bound group, and as dawn approached they'd come under attack from machine guns concealed in a hedgerow about three hundred yards away. Several of the troopers were shot dead at once.

Hunkered low in the field, Dickson had returned fire with his M3 and swiftly realized the German gunners were well outside its effective range. Worse, they seemed to be locked in on the greaser's muzzle flash.

Dickson knew he was in trouble. All he'd managed to accomplish with the weapon was to become a perfect bull's-eye. He would have to cease firing—but as he'd chided himself on landing, you couldn't fight a war without a gun.

Staying low, he scrambled over to one of the troopers who'd been cut down in the grass. He couldn't afford to think about who he'd been or what the bullets had done to him. He couldn't let himself react to the metallic smell of blood coming off his sprawled, limp body to mingle with the smell of the wet grass and soil. The young soldier was dead. The M1 Thompson he'd carried would be of no use to him anymore. And Dickson badly needed it if he wanted to stay alive.

He took the weapon from the trooper's lifeless hands, wiped off the blood, and joined the other paratroopers in returning fire.

The tommy gun worked better than his original weapon. Though it was larger and harder to handle than the greaser, the sheer torrent of ammunition that could pour from its barrel more than compensated for any drawbacks.

The incoming fire finally stopped. Dickson, his two guards, and the paratroopers with whom they'd tagged along moved on through the grass in the diffuse predawn light.

The S-2s still hadn't quite gotten their bearings and remained an unknown distance from the guns at Saint-Martin. But with daylight near, they were hopeful they would spot some useful land-marks and orient themselves.

They dashed from hedgerow to hedgerow, doggedly seeking their objective. As the sun rose over the Cotentin Peninsula on the morning of June 6, it was really all they could do.

7.

Acting Sergeant Jake McNiece didn't just look like an Indian on the warpath, he took a fair amount of pride in being one—or at least in being part Oklahoma Choctaw, on his mother's side. His Irish half was how he'd gotten his name and, by extension, his nickname, "McNasty." But he admitted that he found his Native American birthright had some practical benefits.

Back in England, he'd once used it as a reason to skip reveille, although that hadn't washed with his higher-ups. Nor had the drinking binge he'd gone on afterward in downtown London. That had gotten him a few days in the stockade. But he'd managed to give the MPs who arrested him a beating with their own night-sticks, and that had been pretty satisfying to him . . . especially since *they'd* been beating up on some poor recruit outside a bar when he decided enough was enough and stepped in.

He hadn't been made to stand retreat again, not after taking care of those MPs. In his mind that alone had been worth a stint in the brig.

McNiece didn't give a damn about rules and regulations. He didn't care about discipline or pleasing his officers. He extended his leaves whenever he felt like it and would sometimes disappear from camp for days on end. But guys would follow him anywhere. They trusted him to lead them, and knew he'd never ask them to do anything he wouldn't do himself. That was why he always wound up getting bumped back from sergeant to private, or acting sergeant, after they kicked him down in rank. The Army tolerated him because he was a damn good soldier, and because he knew what it took to energize and mentally prepare men for fighting a war.

The attitude McNiece instilled in the men was pretty basic: You had to be aggressive and ready to kill. The biggest reason he'd enlisted in the paratroopers was because he wanted the chance to go "eyeball-to-eyeball" with a person who wanted to kill him, wanted it to be his personal ability matched against that of the enemy. He hated the thought of being ten miles behind the lines with regular infantry when a German shell dropped down from the clear blue sky and knocked him out of his undershorts.

Paratroopers had a reputation for being crazy, and the scalp locks and face paint McNiece had gotten his men to wear made them look even crazier. Besides being a nod to his Indian background, he figured it would scare the hell out of the Germans. But he also thought the paint worked better as camouflage than trying to find twigs and leaves to stick in their helmets when they were under fire, and would let them blend in with any kind of foliage. That was the practical side of him again.

It was the same kind of thing with the haircut. McNiece would tell people it was an Indian warrior custom back home in Oklahoma, but that was just a line he'd cooked up so he could have some fun with them. The truth was he'd heard about guys getting head and body lice when they went off to fight in Europe, and then read something about a new kind of head mite called scabies that was almost impossible to get rid of because it burrowed under the scalp. Even the name made him want to scratch . . . *scabies*. He figured if he could wash the sides of his head regularly he stood a chance of avoiding an infection.

McNiece's demolitions skills were also checkmarks in his favor. Before he enlisted, he'd been a firefighter for the War Department, and after Pearl Harbor he nailed a job as gang pusher for a construction project at the Pine Bluff Arsenal in Arkansas, where grenades and bombs were being manufactured for the conflict overseas. Drinking after work with the guys who formulated and tested the explosives, he'd picked their brains about the weapons' chemical composition and properties, how they were triggered, and the basic physics and effects of detonations. He had a thorough insider's knowledge of how to use the materials.

His unit's lengthy official name was the 1st Demolitions Section of the Regimental Headquarters Company of the 506th Parachute Infantry Regiment of the 101st Airborne Division, but they would come to be known by the handle the Filthy Thirteen. Some said they'd gotten the name because of their personal hygiene—or lack of it. McNiece happily admitted that they "never took care of their barracks or any other thing." One night while carousing with a buddy who was an Air Force bomber pilot, he'd told him the men had made a blood oath "not to bathe and to remain filthy and dirty until D-Day, when they . . . would be jumping behind enemy lines."

That explanation for the moniker was given in an article about his team in the U.S. military newspaper *Stars and Stripes*. Published two days after the invasion, it had appeared with a photo of two members of the demo section painting each other's face. But as their reputation grew, McNiece and his blood brothers would claim they'd mostly earned the name because they knew how to fight dirtier than the enemy, and because their superiors knew they were a "damned good bunch of soldiers who did a lot more than they were asked to do . . . and sometimes got in trouble for it."

The truth was they got in trouble a lot. Jack Agnew, McNiece's closest buddy on the team, always said that he knew he'd wind up getting arrested whenever he went on weekend leave with "McNasty." But Jake and his platoon of demolitions saboteurs—or demo-sabos—had usually managed to avoid serious punishment for their repeated offenses. As he later put it, "We went AWOL every weekend we wanted to, and we stayed as long as we wanted till we returned back, because we knew they needed us badly for combat. We stole jeeps. We stole trains. We blew up barracks. We blew down trees. We stole the colonel's whiskey and things like that."

On D-Day Minus One, the demo-sabos had been supposed to drop on Drop Zone D, about three miles north of the Douve bridges, but instead they'd been spread out across the flooded marshes without rhyme or reason. McNiece wound up about five miles off target. Other members of his team were still farther away, while a few had dropped closer to the bridges than planned. There hadn't been a single member of his team nearby where he came down.

Alone for the first two hours after he made landfall, McNiece had oriented himself and marched toward his destination carrying—in addition to his standard paratrooper load—thirty-six pounds of Composition C2 plastic explosive, a thousand feet of primer cord, and a collection of blasting caps. Along the way he'd pulled together about ten troopers from assorted units of the 101st and 82nd Divisions. Though some of them were fellow demo-sabos, and three were mortarmen, he didn't ask their specialties or even share the details of his mission, but assured them that if they stuck with him "everything would be okay."

Beamy Beamesderfer was among this group of troopers. Having strayed to the southwest while seeking his regimental objective at La Barquette, he'd gotten mixed up and thought himself heading toward the locks. His confusion was typical of the men in the hodgepodge squad, most of whom were lost and trying to find their units. Still, McNiece had been able to collect three of his blood brothers from the 1st Demo Section—Jack Agnew, Keith Carpenter, and Mike Marquez—during his long march.

Their progress across the inundated fields was slow, their footing treacherous. Each of the mortarmen carried a half dozen rounds of mortars in an apron-style canvas vest that was so heavy it took two soldiers to slip it over his shoulders. McNiece would recall one of the ammunition bearers stepping from the ankle-deep muck into a flooded ditch and sinking like a lead weight into water that was well over his head, the air bubbling from his lungs. As he struggled to claw his way the surface, before he drowned, McNiece "grabbed him and dragged him on out" and then continued toward his destination.

The bridges were unguarded when the men finally reached them at three o'clock in the morning. McNiece thought that was probably because the Germans hadn't expected Allied forces to be roaming that deep behind their lines. He always claimed the biggest advantage to being a paratrooper was that the enemy could only reserve so many troops for the rear, and that meant they were never fully prepared for you. Meanwhile, you could move about at will right in the middle of their forces with surprise in your favor.

Under cover of darkness, the troopers would now prepare the bridges for demolition, planting their charges on the supports, using the mortarmen's shells as improvised casings for the soft, dough-like plastique. There were three bridges in all, two wooden footbridges and the third a large steel bridge with concrete supports. McNiece's orders were to wire all three, then blow the two smaller bridges and try to hold the main one for the troops and vehicles coming up from Utah Beach. However, if the Germans started to cross it from either direction, McNiece was to blow the span with them on it.

Short on demo-sabos, the sergeant set all his tagalongs to the job out of necessity. He wanted it done before daybreak, when the enemy had a better chance of spotting them. But the men without training and experience in the use of explosives faced unexpected risks.

Beamy Beamesderfer, who worked all night wiring the bridges, tremendously underestimated the potency of the C2. In fact, he'd barely heard of the compound until that night. When the demo-sabos blew the footbridges with a shout of *"Fire in the hole!"* he hadn't moved far enough away to escape the explosive shock wave and went flying through the air.

After he was helped to his feet, Beamesderfer took a quick inventory of himself. Though he'd never lost consciousness, he was dizzy and had a bloody nose. There were scratches and cuts all over his body . . . nothing too deep, but they stung. Still, he figured he'd just been shaken up.

It wasn't long before he started to wonder if something more serious might be wrong with him. His nose wouldn't stop bleeding, and he kept spitting blood from his mouth. When the guys asked how he felt, his replies drew some odd glances. At the time, he had no idea he wasn't making sense to them.

Beamesderfer spent the night at the wired bridge as more paratroopers from different units wandered over. He felt pressure in his head and his ears were ringing. Every so often he'd get confused and babble nonsense. Back then he knew close to nothing about head trauma and could not have suspected he was suffering from a severe concussion.

The first Germans came in the morning and would be followed by more as they fled the Allied advance from the beach. Meanwhile, a lieutenant had arrived from the command post and reiterated McNiece's original orders. No enemy soldiers were to cross the bridge.

The band of sixty or so troopers that had assembled there dug in for a fight. It would rage for the next five days.

8.

As the thin light of daybreak filtered down into the ditch, T/5 Richard Lisk stirred for what seemed the first time in hours. He'd stayed perfectly still as enemy patrols tramped past him throughout the night. It had meant ignoring the pain radiating from his broken foot. It had meant ignoring the earthworms, ants, beetles, and other tiny creatures that had slipped from the damp soil to crawl over his face, hair, and hands and inch exploratively under his uniform. He had wanted to stay alive and protect the Eureka unit, and it had required that he lie there for hours without moving a muscle.

It had been a while since he'd discerned any German voices or footsteps. All night he'd heard machine guns cackling in the near distance, and farther toward the coast the rumble of artillery fire. The eruptions were even louder now, and constant, as if the whole world around him was shuddering from a convulsion that would not let go of it. But there was no sound now in the field outside the drainage ditch. Nothing . . . no twittering of birds, no flapping of their wings as they took flight, or rustling of their notched, jerky movements in the hedgerows. The birds had either fled or been stilled as they nervously awakened to the strange thunder of a storm that had blown in without rain.

In this peculiar silence, this complete and utter *absence* of sound, Lisk knew he was alone. He would use the opening, and the light, to take care of things.

Slowly, he raised his head, pushed himself up from the bottom of the ditch, and peered over its lip. There was no one in sight.

He climbed out of the ditch, trying to keep his weight off his injured foot. After he'd emptied his bladder, he knelt down and lifted the homing beacon and its antenna up into the grass. Back at North Witham he'd drilled with the Eureka units blindfolded. He literally knew how to use one and how to demolish it with his eyes closed.

Methodically now he extended the antenna, broke its light-weight segments into small pieces, and tossed them around the field. Then he pulled the det cord—it was made of fishing line—from inside the device, backing away from it as he ran the cord out to its full twenty-five-foot length. He did not want to be standing too close when it blew.

He looked around the field again. An early June field in the lush Norman countryside, bees gathering pollen from wildflowers, butterflies dabbing the air with color.

But there was no birdsong.

His face smeared with dirt, his hair clotted with it, dirt under his fingernails and embedded in the creases of his knuckles, Lisk clenched his fist around the det cord and gave it a hard tug. Heat smacked his cheeks as the Eureka was blasted to pieces amid chuffs of dark gray smoke, its tube-and-wire guts disintegrating from the pressurized explosion, its case fragmenting into an unrecognizable wreck around them. Scraps of twisted metal shot upward and then dropped to the grass. Dials, knobs, and bits of broken glass went zipping everywhere like tiny rockets.

Lisk stood there a moment looking at the demolished unit, the sharp burnt odor in the air stinging his nostrils, reaching all the way to the back of his throat. Then he limped back over to the ditch and slid back down into it. If the Germans found him now, they could go ahead and put him down like a sick dog, but at least they wouldn't get their hands on the homing box.

Time passed. He lay motionless as the blast smoke dissipated and the sky brightened with full morning. Then he heard footsteps approaching and inhaled through his front teeth.

After a moment he heard an American voice call out his name. His comrades had kept their promise to send a medic back for him.

A shot of morphine in his foot anesthetized the pain to the extent that Lisk was able to walk. As the medic moved off with his kit, tending to other soldiers, he went off in search of his unit command post.

Although he didn't locate it at once, he found some glider pilots who were also looking for it and joined them.

They would eventually reach the command post at Mézières, where, that same morning, several of Colonel Pat Cassidy's men were engaging the enemy in the bloodiest of firefights.

9.

As Lisk had huddled at the bottom of the ditch in the hours before dawn, the rest of his Pathfinder stick—along with a handful of survivors from Beamy Beamesderfer's plane—had marked off the landing zone for fifty-two Waco gliders that had flown over the coastline in groups of four, each glider towed by a Dakota.

The Chicago mission, as it was dubbed, had a broad-ranging purpose. Forty-four of the lightweight canvas-and-wood aircraft were transporting two batteries of an antiaircraft battalion, sixteen 57mm field guns, twenty-five Willys jeeps and small trucks, a bulldozer, and almost fifteen tons of combined ammunition and equipment. Eight gliders carried engineers, signalmen, an antitank platoon, and an entire surgical unit from the 326th Airborne Medical Company to staff a field outpost. All told there were 148 troopers aboard the Wacos.

The lead glider had been named after the *Fighting Falcon*, the first aircraft of its type to be constructed by the industrious Gibson Refrigerator Company in Greenville, Michigan. Painted on the pilot's side of the nose was a giant representation of the 101st Airborne's Screaming Eagle insignia. A similarly large-scale American flag was emblazoned on the opposite side.

At the controls of *Fighting Falcon* was Colonel Mike Murphy, the Army's most seasoned glider pilot, a former barnstormer who'd once drawn breathless wows by landing customized planes upside down at air shows. Lieutenant John Butler, his copilot, sat beside him in the cockpit. The assistant division commander of the 101st Airborne, Brigadier General Don F. Pratt, was behind them in the front passenger seat of a lashed-down jeep, wearing his combat helmet and Mae West vest, using a flashlight to pore over the classified dispatches stuffing a big leather briefcase on his knees. Beside the jeep, Pratt's aide-de-camp, Lieutenant John May, was crammed in with some five-gallon jerry cans of gasoline that would fuel the jeep along the Cotentin's roads, having been squeezed out of the vehicle by the equipment stowed aboard it. The items included several powerful radio sets the general had brought for his divisional command post—but they would never be used.

Don Pratt was about to become the first and highest-ranking officer on either side of the war to die in the D-Day invasion.

Ironically, he was a late addition to Chicago. Early in the invasion planning, Pratt had received the assignment of leading the seaborne invasion fleet, but he'd coaxed Major General Maxwell Taylor, chief of the 101st, into letting him hit Normandy with the advance airborne element so he could have a head start organizing the ground forces. Although he'd wanted to come in with the paratroopers, Pratt had never earned jump quals, leaving a glider arrival as his only option.

Mike Murphy was likewise a last-minute pick for the operation. In England to train glider pilots for the D-Day invasion, he'd been disappointed to find out he wasn't slated to fly across the Channel with them. But his opening came when he got wind of General Pratt's change of plans. Like the general, he'd lobbied his superior officer, explaining that it was important for him to get a close-up look at how the Wacos performed in combat. His best argument would be unstated, though: The Army would want to be certain that someone of Pratt's rank had the best glider pilot available for his flight, and Murphy knew his expertise was unsurpassed.

While General Pratt was said to have been eager to fly aboard a Waco, his staff worried about the risk to his life. Without consulting him, they ordered a layer of steel-plate armor installed at the bottom of the fuselage to shield him from enemy ground fire— and arranged for him sit atop a parachute pack in the jeep. The armor not only added hundreds of pounds of weight to an aircraft already carrying a 2,300-pound vehicle and other heavy cargo, but threw the distribution of that weight dangerously off balance.

Murphy only heard about the *Fighting Falcon*'s ad hoc belly armor before takeoff, and it made him concerned about the glider's airworthiness. He had previously ordered an experimental crash-resistant nose placed on a glider and felt that was all the added protection it could safely handle. But with everything set to go at the airfield, no one was inclined to request a last-minute change of plans.

At 1:19 on the morning of June 6, a C-47 with the *Fighting Falcon* in tow had left England on schedule, with the other Chicago planes and gliders following at thirty-second intervals. Murphy's extra weight load created problems from the start, forcing his tow ship to use a huge amount of runway to get him airborne—and when the pilot finally did take wing, he'd had more difficulties staying level. It was, he would recall, like trying to fly a freight train.

The lift met little resistance overflying the Channel Islands at two thousand feet, but things got hot over the French coastline as enemy guns opened up on them. In the *Falcon*'s pilot seat, Murphy heard bullets ricochet off the jeep and penetrate his wings and fuselage with a sound that reminded him of popcorn popping. But with no engines or fuel tanks that could ignite, the rounds passed through the canvas without doing critical harm.

The situation worsened when the heavier antiaircraft guns awakened below. Wishing they could crawl into their helmets, the glider pilots flew through fluid streams of flak that were "beautiful yet frightening, orange fireballs coming up through the air and arching off in a curve. Always the fire was directed at the tow ship ahead, with its exhausts belching bright blue flames." As the lift settled into its final approach route, the German AA gunners lit bonfires on the ground to warm themselves against the chill, damp weather, and the orange glare had the secondary effect of blinding the pilots. With their eyes taxed by all these visual distractions, many of them would never know how they managed to stay on course.

It was about 4 A.M. when Murphy saw a green light in the astrodome of his towplane, signaling that they'd reached their destination outside the village of Hiesville.

"*So long,*" he said to the transport. He could hear German machine-gun fire through the roar of the wind outside the cockpit and was thinking he'd had his fill of it.

Hitting his towline release knob, he exchanged a relieved glance with his copilot. It wasn't just the gunfire that had worn on their nerves. The glider's added, misplaced weight had made it buck and shimmy in the air practically from takeoff, and they'd spent more than two and a half hours wrestling with their controls to keep it steady. Coupled with the strain of having to fly through walls of flak, the effort had left them mentally and physically tired out, their shoulders sore with fatigue, their arms and legs stiffly cramped.

Despite his weariness, Murphy decided to give himself some extra hang time so he could get a feel for how to land the unstable aircraft. The very rules he'd helped institute for glider landings required a pilot to stay level as he slowed to his descent speed, but he would now make an exception, turn sharply to the left, and bring the *Fighting Falcon* up into a steep climb.

His maneuver worked like a charm.

Although daylight was still a couple of hours off, the high, full moon clearly limned the geography below in its shining silver light. Murphy could see the outlines of the Norman fields and hedgerows he'd studied on his maps, and even spotted a railroad track he'd known would be a mile and a half from the LZ. He and the other glider pilots would now find out what the 101's paratroopers had already discovered: The trees in the hedgerows around the landing zone were much taller than their briefings had led them to believe. Although they'd been told the highest trees were forty feet tall, many of the poplars bordering the field in the thick bocage towered sixty feet above the ground.

This might have presented a hazard for the pilots under some circumstances. But the Pathfinders who'd landed ahead of the glider lift had perfectly defined the runways. Marked on a downhill slope with a lighted T, Murphy's was between a thousand and twelve hundred feet long. He normally required much less than that—two or three hundred feet, tops—to brake to a halt. The large built-in margin for error convinced him he'd have an easy landing.

His achy muscles forgotten in his concentration, he made his descent without a hitch, though he'd picked up a tailwind that nudged his velocity up to about seventy miles an hour, ten miles over the optimum final approach speed. Just before touchdown, he would see the lift's number two glider bank in for its landing to his right. Then he felt his wheels bump to the ground.

As he'd practiced countless times, Murphy hauled back on the brake lever and lowered the glider's nose to trim its speed—but to his stunned surprise it continued to slide over the rain-slicked grass without slowing down. Two hundred feet, three hundred . . . four, five . . . *eight hundred* . . .

Murphy's face pulled tight with dismay. His machine wasn't stopping; its poorly distributed extra weight sustained its downhill momentum. He could see the hedgerow coming up on him like a dark, solid wall. Bracing for a collision, he looked down the slope, saw a column of treaded vehicles with blackout lights through a break in the foliage, and knew they were Germans—they had to be, since he'd been told no American vehicles would roll before dawn. He snapped his head around to warn whoever could hear him, but his voice failed to reach his lips, and the best he could muster was as a hoarse, ragged whisper.

Then the *Fighting Falcon* plowed into the hedgerow's five-and-a-half-foot-high earthen embankment and struck a tree with a loud, rending crash that shook the ground. Belted into his seat,

Murphy was tossed helplessly back and forth as the glider's windscreen shattered in front of him. He felt pain jolt through every bone in his body, and then was hanging partway from the aircraft's window into the shrubbery, its nose section's steel-reinforced frame crunched around him in a twisted mass.

The next few seconds were a sickening blur. Dazed and in agony, Murphy glanced over to his right and saw Butler's mangled, bloodied body wedged into the floor of the cockpit. He'd taken the brunt of the impact with the tree and been crushed between the jeep and its trunk, a branch driven through his skull like a javelin. Still strapped into the vehicle's passenger seat, General Pratt showed no visible injuries. But his head was bent forward to his chest and he wasn't moving—not encouraging signs. Barely able to move himself, Murphy was unable to check on the condition of Lieutenant May, the general's aide who'd been outside the jeep in the cargo section.

A wave of dizziness came and went. He was dimly aware that Glider Number 2 had slammed into the hedges about a hundred and fifty feet to his left. Meanwhile, the armored vehicles he'd spotted before the crash were still visible through the hedge. There were five of them, or five that he could count, German soldiers sitting with their legs over the vehicles' sides and rifles across their laps, peering into the field where the gliders had landed.

His legs pinned by the twisted steel tubing, his upper body dangling into the hedges, Murphy watched two of the enemy soldiers jump down off the vehicles and then walk along the line of shrubs toward the glider, outthrust flashlights in their hands.

He remained perfectly still, trying not to breathe as they reached it, briefly held their flashes over him, then slipped them inside the aircraft and swept their pale yellow beams around its broken interior.

After a hurried inspection, they straightened and tramped back to their vehicles. Murphy waited some more, listening. Minutes later, he heard the armored wagons rumble off into the night. Whether the Germans believed everyone inside the glider had been killed, or were concerned about the arriving Allied planes, they had wanted no part of sticking around the field.

Murphy didn't budge for another several minutes, to be certain they'd moved on. Then he began trying to wriggle free of the glider's cockpit.

The pain in his lower half almost unbearable, he screwed himself out of the aircraft a little at a time, gripping its tangled frame with both hands for support. But he'd no sooner stood up than his legs gave way underneath him and he went tumbling down into a shallow ditch.

Murphy lay there briefly, the air knocked from his lungs. Then he dug his fingers into the side of the ditch and began struggling to claw his way out.

He'd almost done so when Lieutenant May arrived holding a submachine gun. The aide had shuffled behind the jeep seconds before the crash, hoping it would absorb some of the shock. His desperate attempt at survival had worked; he was bruised and badly shaken up, but otherwise unharmed. When the Germans had come with their flashlights, he'd done the same as Murphy and faked being dead.

The news he brought about General Pratt wasn't good. Before leaving the glider, he'd checked him for a pulse and hadn't detected one. But he'd thought it possible he could have missed it in his shock and distress.

If Murphy and the general's aide knew one thing for certain, it was that the wreck would need to be guarded until medical assistance arrived. As May rushed back off to find help, Murphy drew his Colt service pistol from his holster—his M1 had gotten bent into a U-shape in the crash—and kept his own lookout from the side of the ditch. He did not trust the Germans in the armored vehicles to stay away.

Captain Charles Van Gorder, a surgeon with the 326th Medical Company who'd been aboard the number two lift, would find him crawling along outside the ditch with his .45 at the ready, dragging his legs behind him. Van Gorder had run over to him after having examined the occupants of his aircraft and determined none were seriously injured.

After seeing the *Falcon*'s condition, he hadn't expected its passengers to have fared as well. Wrapped around the tree it had hit, the stricken glider had been reduced to an unrecognizable pile of debris.

Crouching over Murphy, Van Gorder knew instantly that his legs were broken—one of them with a compound fracture, its splintered femur poking out of the torn flesh. His left knee had also been horribly torn up. The surgeon's first thought was that he would die from shock and blood loss before he could reach triage. With that in mind, he'd offered to relieve his suffering with a palliative shot of morphine.

Murphy refused. "I want to stay alert," he said, "so I can shoot Germans."

Van Gorder left the syringe inside his medical kit.

By now Lieutenant May had returned to the *Falcon* with a detail of paratroopers. Leaving them to stand watch, he trotted over to Van Gorder and asked him to take a look at the general. The doctor quickly walked the short distance to the wreckage and tried to examine him, but he couldn't work his arms through the mashed tubing. Stripping off his gear, he finally managed to squeeze in and check Pratt and Butler's vital signs.

Neither man had a pulse or a heartbeat. They were dead.

May's spirits sank. While there had been little doubt that Butler was gone, he'd been clinging to the slender hope that the general was merely unconscious. But Van Gorder's inspection revealed he'd died of severe whiplash. Though Pratt was a short man, the parachute pack had raised him up high enough so that when the jeep rammed forward into the cockpit, his head struck a crossbar of the glider's framework, snapping his neck back. The supposed precautions his staff had taken against threats to his life in the air had been the direct cause of his death on landing.

Van Gorder now returned to Murphy and splinted his broken legs using whatever materials he could gather. The pilot was eventually removed to a field hospital the 326th Airborne Medical established at a nearby château. Sometime later on D-Day, a group of paratroopers arrived for General Pratt's body, wrapped him in an American flag, and buried him near the wreckage of the *Fighting Falcon*. There was no traditional gun salute out of concern it would draw attention from the enemy.

The pilot of the number two glider, Lieutenant Victor Warriner, remained in the field for hours afterward. Curiously peering into the ruined glider, he noticed a helmet on the floor. When he saw the single white star in front, he knew it had been the general's.

He reached in, lifted the helmet out, and held it in his hands a moment, thinking he might hang on to it as a war memento. But then he reconsidered. The idea just didn't sit right inside him. It belonged where it belonged.

Carefully, Warriner bent back into the glider, set the helmet back down where he'd found it, and walked off.

Somehow, that made him feel better.

CHAPTER THREE

1.

Staff Sergeant Harrison Summers, B/502, 101st Airborne, had been in an ugly state of mind when he'd joined Colonel Pat Cassidy's march toward Objective W-X-Y-Z. Before hooking up with Cassidy, his misdropped stick had landed near the town of Sainte-Mère-Église in one of the areas the 82nd Airborne had been sent to take. When he and another of the staff sergeants, Roy Nickrent, walked past the village church, they'd seen dead American paratroopers hanging from the trees where they came down, their chutes still on. Some of them had been shot, others bayoneted. In some cases they had suffered a variety of different wounds. One of the jumpers had been burned up by a flamethrower, and Summers's fellow sergeant had recognized him as one of his closest friends. The horrible appearance of his remains, and the smell of his charred flesh, would leave permanent scars on their memories.

Reaching the W-X-Y-Z compound shortly before 6:30 A.M., Summers and the men rushed the first of the stone houses with Cassidy after taking a wild gunshot from inside it. A room-to-room sweep turned up no enemy soldiers, and the house was quickly declared clear and turned into a command post—though two Germans would be flushed out of hiding later that day after being secreted away by the property's French landlady, who said they'd been "kind" to her.

Cassidy then led a detail to the Saint-Martin coastal battery position and found it a deserted ruin, exactly as Captain Lillyman had described. After several unsuccessful tries, his radioman made contact with the 4th Infantry Division at Utah Beach and gave them word that the guns were no longer a threat to the landing craft. It was the first communication between the airborne and seaborne invasion forces in the area.

With the guns no longer a concern, Cassidy planned to establish a tight security perimeter around the CP and "build a small defensive base" at the crossroads of Saint-Martin-de-Varreville and Mézières to "keep the Germans from breaking through to the beach."

His other immediate priority was to clear out the W-X-Y-Z barracks compound a few hundred yards west of his command post. He had no idea if it was still occupied, but the absence of German defenders at the CP and gun battery made him hopeful it would be similarly emptied. Before leaving to inspect the battery, he sent Sergeant Summers out toward the buildings with a patrol of about fifteen soldiers. It was a smaller group than he'd have ideally chosen, but he was short on manpower and they were all the troopers he could spare.

Summers's leadership of the patrol would be hamstrung from the start. The narrow road to the compound was hemmed in by shrubs and trees, preventing the men from spreading out at its flank—and forcing the members of the squad to walk in a single file, which made them nervous about an ambush. The motley assortment was also made up of soldiers from different units who were strangers to one another and the twenty-five-year-old sergeant, who "didn't know a single man in the detail." They hadn't trained together and developed the bonds of trust and friendship that helped forge a cohesive fighting unit.

At about nine o'clock in the morning, Summers saw the first farmhouse just up ahead, turned to give the men instructions, and saw them hesitate. At that moment he made the snap decision to storm the buildings himself, figuring that if he went ahead and set an example the others would follow.

His Thompson at the ready, he went stalking toward the two-story building—and that was when the Germans opened up on the troopers and sent them scrambling for cover in the ditches on either side of the road. Raising his head, Summers could see their semiautomatic fire coming from the first floor, where they had fabricated loopholes in the structure's thick stone wall.

A soft-spoken coal miner from rural West Virginia, he would never be able to articulate what came over him right at that moment. He simply decided the job had to be done, pushed to his feet, walked to the farmhouse's back door with the tommy gun at his waist, and kicked it in, spraying the room on the other side with fire.

As four of the Germans dropped from the sustained volley, a number of others and some civilians went running through another door into the hedges, heading toward the second house in the cluster. Summers followed them there, smashed in the door, and stared inside.

The room was empty except for a sick-looking child. The sergeant would never recollect whether the face staring back at him from the bed belonged to a boy or girl. He was in an adrenaline-washed haze, a state of near abstraction, and mostly took in the kid's frailty and defenselessness. A small, sick, innocent child looking at a man in a strange uniform. A soldier with a gun in his hand, a face that was smeared black, and killing in his eyes.

It briefly stopped Summers cold. Then enemy rounds began pouring from the third farmhouse, about fifty yards away. Snapped back into the reality of what he'd come to do, Summers tore his eyes from the bed and charged out the door, dashing up the road toward the next house, zigzagging to avoid the fire.

Behind him in the ditch, a young private named William Burt found himself stirred by the sergeant's courage and realized he couldn't just watch him go it alone. Crawling out of the ditch with his BAR light machine gun, Burt hastily set up the weapon, stretched out on the ground behind it, and began triggering a hail of suppressive fire, aiming for the gun ports in the farmhouse wall.

That blinded the German soldiers crouched behind them. Their heads ducked, unable see their moving target, they fired scatter-shot at Summers through the ports, raking the bushes and trimming the leaves off the trees above his head.

The sergeant took full advantage of their misplaced volleys. With a final charge toward the house, he kicked in the door with a booted foot, the tommy gun chattering in his hand even as it flung wide open.

The Germans in the room never saw him coming. He would have time to notice six men in coal scuttle helmets still shooting through the loopholes before he took them out with one broad sweep of his gun.

Summers stood in the entrance for a long moment afterward, his eyes moving about the room. He saw blood dripping down from the walls to the floorboards and spreading in pools under the bodies of the soldiers. He heard their delayed muscle spasms, the involuntary twitching of their arms and legs. He smelled death in the confined air. Before that morning he had never fired a rifle except in practice. Now he'd killed almost a dozen men in the span of minutes. It had already exhausted him . . . and there were still seven buildings to clear.

Sometime before he reemerged, Summers's squad climbed up out of the ditches and joined Private Burt in firing their weapons at the compound's fourth building—a small, single-story structure. Under cover of the guns, Summers resumed his charge, sprinting over to the door and shouldering all his weight against it.

He realized too late that it was partly open. Stumbling forward on his own unchecked momentum, the sergeant crashed hard to the floor, the wind knocked out of him.

To his good fortune the interior of the outbuilding's single room was empty. He rose to his feet, catching his breath. Then he turned back outside and sank to the doorstep in exhaustion.

Summers sat there, smoked a Lucky Strike, and took pulls of warm water from his canteen. At one point some of the men came over and replenished his ammunition. There was no sign of the enemy. If there were more of them in the compound, they would have to be flushed out of hiding.

About half an hour later, Summers saw someone he didn't know approaching the house, raised his tommy gun from his side . . . and then lowered it. The man was wearing an American paratrooper's uniform. A tall, lank captain with an 82nd Airborne patch on his sleeve, he explained that he'd misdropped into a nearby apple orchard, wandered toward the buildings, and seen the sergeant storming in and out of them with his tommy gun ablaze. He hadn't noticed the rest of his squad in the ditch.

By now Summers felt rested. He got to his feet and told the captain he was ready to move on toward the next building, a large, two-floor manor house standing about a quarter mile across the road.

The captain fell in next to him. "I'll go with you," he said, and had barely started toward the house when a rifle shot cracked the air and he crumpled dead to the ground, the front of his uniform splashed with red.

Summers glanced numbly down at the man's body. A bullet had penetrated his heart. It had happened so fast, he'd never even gotten his name—but there was no time to think about it. The shot had come from the manor, and he had no available cover. Not unless he backtracked toward the house he'd just left, or scrambled into a ditch.

He didn't like either option. It would do no good to be pinned down. Instead, he sprinted toward the manor, stitching evasively to the left and right. Following his lead, Private Burt moved up with a couple of other men, shooting at the outside of the house from the roadside brush, trying to draw off the sniper's fire.

One of the men, Private John Camien, had seen enough. He burst from the hedge and came up alongside Summers as he ran.

With Private Burt covering them, they quickly reached the manor, coming to a halt outside its door.

"Why are you doing it?" Camien asked in a New York accent.

"I can't tell you," Summers said.

"What about the others?"

"They don't seem to want to fight, and I can't make them," Summers said. "So I've got to finish it."

Camien nodded and hefted his carbine. "Okay," he said. "I'm with you."

Summers burst in the door, Camien standing guard outside as he conducted a furious room-to-room search, cutting down six German soldiers as others fled the building and surrendered to the men in the ditches. They would take turns entering the next three buildings, switching weapons, killing more than two dozen enemy soldiers. Burt continued to move up the road along the side of the ditch, harassing the defenders at the gun ports with his light machine gun, making it impossible for them to take accurate aim at the two paratroopers.

There were now two buildings left in the compound, the closest a stately old château with white-shuttered windows and neat low hedges in front. Summers and Camien ran the hundred fifty yards to it, the sergeant going in, his companion watching the entrance.

Summers crashed through the door, found two empty rooms, and then stared into a third large room with astonishment. The Germans had converted it into a mess hall, and about fifteen of them were at a long wooden table eating their breakfasts, seemingly oblivious to the gunfire that had been tearing through the compound. He looked at their faces for a suspended moment and saw them staring back at him over their eggs, sausage, and steaming cups of coffee. Anyone with a working pair of ears would have heard the noise outside. He couldn't comprehend it. How much could they have liked their chow?

Summers opened fire with his tommy gun even as the silverware clattered from their hands and they went groping for their weapons. His brain in a kind of haze, he held his finger on the trigger and relentlessly chopped away until every last one of them was dead, the room transformed into a slaughterhouse, blood everywhere, bodies sprawling on the floor and draped over the tables and benches.

It was all over in a minute. Summers felt the heat coming off his gun barrel as he lowered it, got his cigarettes back out of his pocket with a trembling hand, and shook one out.

When Camien entered the house, he found the sergeant crouched on his knees and puffing on a Lucky Strike, smoke streaming from his nostrils. Although he looked tired to the bone, his features were set and coldly dispassionate. There was one last building to clear.

Summers finished his smoke and led Camien outside to reconnoiter it. They found a tall hedgerow with a thick dirt embankment and crawled up to peer through the foliage.

The structure, another two-story farmhouse with a large wooden shed connected to it, was on a knoll surrounded by many yards of flat, open ground. The Germans at the gun ports had an elevated vantage and clear lines of sight on all sides. It would make it easy for them to target any attacker coming on across the field. Studying it from behind the hedgerow, Summers was convinced they couldn't rush it as they had the other buildings.

They were about to get some unexpected support. Down the road, Colonel Cassidy had heard the gunfire coming from W-X-Y-Z and sent additional forces into the compound as men from different units trickled into his command post. He had been tempted to lead them himself, but with the fighting having heated up at his roadblocks and a stream of wounded infantrymen and German prisoners flowing into the CP, he felt he needed to stay back there to coordinate things.

His first group of reinforcements entered the compound to the left of Summers's platoon. Met with a combination of sniper and small arms fire from the farmhouse, seven of them were killed and the rest sent scrambling for cover. As Summers had feared, the Germans' position on the high ground gave them a deadly advantage over the troopers.

It was Private Burt whose brainstorm tilted those circumstances in another direction. Firing away at the farmhouse with his machine gun, he'd spotted a large pile of hay beside its attached shed. Almost at once, it occurred to him that he might be able to flush the enemy soldiers out of the main building—or at least make it harder for them to stay at their gun ports.

Replacing the BAR's standard .50-caliber ammunition with tracers, he took aim at the haystack and inundated it with pyrotechnic rounds. The burning chemicals inside them ignited the dry stack at once, the flames completely swallowing it up and then spreading across to the shed. In minutes it was ablaze, the smoke and fire leaping up the side of the farmhouse to chase the enemy soldiers away from their ports.

Burt's plan had done the trick, but he was about to get even better dividends than he could have foreseen. What he hadn't known was that the Germans had been using the shed as a heavy ammo dump—and it was stocked with live artillery shells. As the

fire tore through its planks, the ammunition inside began to deto-
nate, a chain of explosions that flushed about thirty enemy soldiers
out of the structure and onto the hillside. Caught between the
group that had come with Summers and Cassidy's reinforcements,
they were shot down as they bolted from the door.

The soldiers inside the farmhouse remained holed up, though,
hoping its ancient two-and-a-half-foot-thick stone walls could keep
out the flames as well as it had thus far repelled the Americans'
gunfire. And they might have if not for one of Cassidy's late reinforcements.

Sergeant Roy Nickrent was the trooper who had hiked with
Summers from their drop zone, and seen his good friend's disfigured
remains in a tree while passing through the village of Sainte-Mère-
Église. Trained at using the bazooka he'd brought with him—he
called it his type of work—his mood was no more forgiving toward
the Germans than it had been when he arrived at the command post.

Finding a good spot behind the mess hall, he knelt, balanced the
launcher on his shoulder, and fired two shots at the farmhouse to
get his range. The first fell short. The second hit the stone wall of
the building near its base. Systematically making adjustments, he
fired four more charges.

The sixth finned rocket leaped from the tube to the roof of the
farmhouse and spun down into it with a blast that reverberated
across the fields. Seconds later, Nickrent saw black smoke spewing
out of the hole.

Fifty Germans were killed as they fled the building, and thirty
others were taken prisoners of war. The total number of dead and
captured enemy soldiers after five hours of combat at W-X-Y-Z
would come to more than a hundred and fifty.

Harrison Summers would later call the whole thing kind of crazy, and never really felt too good about it—in fact, the events of that morning would sometimes make him feel cold and dirty when he thought about them on the far side of midnight. It was as if he'd lost his mind, lost his reasoning. He hadn't cared if he got killed or not, but he figured if he went, he was going to take some Germans with him.

Watching the last of the compound's buildings get eaten by flames, his weapon perched on his shoulder, Roy Nickrent, perhaps better than anyone, had understood.

2.

At six-thirty in the evening on D-Day, about twelve hours after the Allied seaborne assault commenced, the thirty-two gliders and towplanes of a second glider serial—codenamed Keokuk—left Aldermaston Airfield southwest of London for the Cotentin Peninsula. Flown by the 434th Troop Carrier Group, the lift was on a mission to reinforce the 101st Airborne with antiaircraft guns, medical and signal personnel, jeeps, and other vital supplies.

Despite having fewer gliders, Keokuk's total payload was roughly equivalent to the Chicago mission's cargo. This was because the British Airspeed Horsa used for the operation was much larger than the CG-4A Waco, carrying double the number of troops—thirty as compared to twelve—and a heavier freight—8,586 pounds versus

3,750 pounds. Its wooden construction made it sturdier, if less maneuverable, than the flimsy canvas-and-tubular-steel American version, and its hemp-rope tow harness was attached to both wings (rather than just the nose) to give it greater stability in flight. But the most significant difference between the airlifts was that Keokuk was scheduled for early evening, when it was hoped the glider pilots would benefit from the available daylight as they guided their big Horsas toward a suitable landing field.

It would be Frank Lillyman's Pathfinders who prepared the LZ. After helping to set up roadblocks at Cassidy's northern perimeter, they had gradually made their way to the divisional command post established at Hiesville by personnel from the Chicago lift. There they got some rest, took on ammo and provisions, and hiked out to mark the nearby fields where the Keokuk gliders were to come down.

Overlapping Chicago's landing zones, the area had gotten increasingly dangerous as small groups of German snipers and machine-gunners stole into its hedgerows and farm buildings, pressing in on the airborne command post. Troops from a battalion of Georgian enlistees—former POWs who'd chosen to fight for Hitler's war machine rather than starve to death in its prison camps—were also rolling down the main road from the village of Turqueville to the northeast, where the enemy had built up a sizeable combat force of soldiers, armored vehicles, and artillery guns, housing them in massive concrete blockhouses. The reinforcements were massing for a single purpose; it was here outside Hiesville that the Germans planned to build a defensive line against the Allied troops moving in from the beach.

After arriving from the CP, Lillyman filmed the wreckage of General Pratt's glider for the U.S. Army archives, then went to work on the LZ with his crew and a few other paratroopers he'd assembled from different units. Their first order of business was to find a field that was large enough for the Horsas and had been cleared of Rommel's asparagus and other lethal obstacles. The Pathfinders would again utilize their luminous Holophane panels and a Eureka beacon in laying out the site, but this time they added green smoke pots to their array of signaling equipment. The colored smoke, which wouldn't have been visible to the aircrews during the night landings, would give Keokuk's pilots another visual aid to home in on.

Their landing zone chosen, the Pathfinders arranged their Holophanes in the familiar T pattern, setting the radar beacon at the north end of the T and the smoke pots in the middle, where Lillyman was positioned. Standing guard as the trailblazers built their runway, their security detail took almost no enemy fire from the hedges—but the silence would prove deceptive. Hidden in the trees and bushes, the Germans had planned a deadly welcome for the gliders, lying in wait until they were within range of their small arms and rockets.

Shortly before nine o'clock, the Keokuk gliders crossed Utah Beach, cut loose from their C-47 tugs, and descended on the peninsula. As they neared the ground, the enemy guns came alive beneath them, throwing a sleet of ammunition up at their wings and fuselages. The pilots dropped fast, their Horsas smacking into the trees and hedges, some breaking apart as they hit at a high speed. Incredibly, less than a fourth of those aboard were killed or seriously hurt in the crashes.

But the Germans were quick to close in. The crewmen and passengers exiting the shattered aircraft with their injured flight mates—either on foot or in the jeeps that had been part of the air train's cargo—were at once met by ripples of machine-gun and Mk-40 burp-gun fire and chased across the fields by mortar rounds. Their objective was to reach the command post less than a mile off, a simple plan in concept that would have to be executed with a concealed enemy firing at them from all sides.

Frank Lillyman was still at the T when he saw one of the gliders slam to earth a short distance away and raced off in the direction of the crash, his squad following behind. As the Pathfinders emerged from an opening in the foliage and saw the demolished glider on the ground, they instantly realized it was under fire from the hedgerow. Hidden in the bushes, the Germans were shooting at the glider's occupants as they tried to evacuate, barraging them with machine-gun fire and rocket launchers.

Lillyman and his men spread out in the hedges along their side of the field, aimed their weapons at the enemy gun nest, and opened up on it, drawing its volleys away from the beleaguered glider crew. With fire coming at them from different angles, the Germans may have thought themselves outnumbered, and they broke off the engagement, fleeing through the vegetation.

But even as they made their retreat, Lillyman heard the characteristic *brrrrp* of an Mk-40 firing a short burst and felt a sudden, biting heat across his arm.

Hearing one of the men shout his name as if from a distance, he looked down himself, at his chewed up uniform sleeve, saw the blood welling out of it in pulses, and knew he'd been shot.

Then his legs gave out underneath him and he went down hard, a chunk of shrapnel from a detonated mortar shell slicing into his face as he hit the ground.

3.

It was not until late in the morning of June 7 that Buck Dickson and his S-2s found their way to Colonel Cassidy's 1st Battalion command post at Mézières. They were tired, bedraggled, and famished after more than thirty-six hours of hedgerow fighting beside groups of paratroopers from the 101st and 86th, all while trying to locate the coastal battery position that had been their objective.

At the CP, Dickson reported in to Cassidy, telling him exactly what had happened to him after getting separated from the Pathfinders, only to learn from the colonel that the German gun emplacements at Saint-Martin-de-Varreville had been abandoned. Possibly the Germans had fled after the 394th Bombardment Group's first run in mid-May, taking three of the four long-range cannons with them. The two hundred enemy troops billeted at W-X-Y-Z had, of course, remained entrenched until the day before—but Cassidy's men had thoroughly cleaned them out.

Dickson digested that without saying much. It was an odd feeling. His team had spent every minute since their jump resolutely fighting toward a goal that already had been accomplished.

After his debriefing, he left the command post and went a few hundred yards east along the road to where the artillery guns had stood, walking past the wounded paratroopers in their bloodied uniforms and bandages, the German prisoners of war, the soldiers coming in for orders, supplies, and first aid. When he reached the bombed out field, he strode across the rubble to one of the empty concrete artillery bunkers and stared quietly west toward Utah Beach, where Headquarters had feared the big guns would be trained. From his vantage point he could not see the ocean or the dunes where the men had come ashore. But they were out there.

Dickson wasn't sure quite how long he'd been standing alone in the sun when someone touched his shoulder. Startled, he turned his head and saw that his old friend from Western Maryland University, Ed "Frosty" Peters, had come up beside him unnoticed. Peters and Dickson had been roommates at school and then some. Both had been in the ROTC program, and Frosty was captain of the football team on which Dickson earned varsity honors.

Now, two and a half years after graduation, Peters was a captain with the United States Army. As chief of the 506th PIR's regimental headquarters, he'd been tabbed for the jump at Drop Zone C, near Vierville, to the southwest.

Recovering from his surprise, Dickson met Frosty's grin with one of his own and grabbed his elbows. Then they flung out their arms and embraced—big, fond, wholehearted, *crushing* bear hugs. Dickson didn't know what his old college pal was doing there in the field and was so pleased to see him he didn't bother to ask. A lot of soldiers from different units were passing through the command post, and he just figured Frosty was one of them.

They spoke happily in the quiet, sun-washed field. Neither man talked about his flight across the Channel, or his jump, or the combat he'd experienced afterward; Dickson didn't think he ought to mention any of it right then. Their encounter here felt like a gift of sorts, a brief, welcome respite from the bloodshed everywhere around them. He wanted it to remain that way while it lasted, and sensed Frosty did too.

So instead they made some cheerful small talk, reminisced about old times at Western MD, and exchanged bits of news about their former classmates from the officers' program, discussing which branches of the military different guys had wound up serving in and where this one or the other was stationed.

After about ten minutes, though, Frosty's face turned serious.

"Well," he said, "I'd better be getting back to my men."

Dickson nodded. "Okay, take care of yourself," he said. Then it occurred to him that Peters would have established his own regimental command post by now—and that it must be relatively close by for him to have walked over from it. "Where's your CP?" he asked.

Peters started walking away. "Over there," he said, motioning across the field. "Behind those trees."

Dickson watched him depart, his gaze following his slow walk toward the hedgerows until he disappeared in their long afternoon shadows. Talking to his friend had given him a real lift after the pure hell of the previous night . . . and it really was quite a coincidence to have met him there in the gun field. The whole thing seemed kind of dreamlike, although he knew it was no dream.

It was only after he'd rotated back to England in July that Dickson learned his friend had been shot to death on June 6, the day before their encounter, while storming an enemy gun position up near his DZ. But he would go to his grave bristling at any suggestion he'd imagined seeing Frosty Peters that day.

"I knew that man well! We *hugged* each other," he would say when summoning up his recollections of the Normandy invasion.

No one who knew the sensible, levelheaded Dickson would have questioned him.

4.

It had been a grueling, bloody five days for Jake McNiece, Beamy Beamesderfer, and all the other troopers at the Douve River Bridge.

German infantrymen retreating from the invasion forces on Utah Beach had tried crossing it twice in the first forty-eight hours, but both times the Americans on the embankments of the elevated causeways cut them down. Then, on the third day, U.S. Mustangs flew in, started carpet bombing the area, and took out a chunk of the bridge.

As McNiece later recalled, the pilots had an order to release their extra bombs after their missions. "They were not supposed to return to the runway with live bombs because an accident might destroy ten other planes." Probably, he surmised, they'd thought the soldiers they saw below were the enemy. He remembered feeling great fear during the runs, then a sense of calm. The men on the ground were powerless to do anything but "wait for the bombs to fall."

Even after the bridge was destroyed, the Germans kept coming from the beaches. With nowhere else to go as the Allies pushed inland, they would charge the flooded marshes trying to escape, calf- and knee-deep in water. Although vastly outnumbered, the American soldiers held the high ground and kept chopping them down.

McNiece had figured out that one way to avoid getting killed was to stay on the move. The Germans would home in on your fire after a while if you stayed in one place, so he would raise his head up above the embankment, trigger a burst into a group of them, duck, and move on to another spot. He spent most of the next few days doing that and killing Germans. Meanwhile more lost paratroopers and survivors from decimated sticks kept wandering in.

On the fifth day, the enemy soldiers finally stopped coming. The American units that had driven them from the beach arrived, and they'd been pressed in on two sides. Hundreds of them lay dead or wounded in the marsh.

When the shooting ended, McNiece and Jack Agnew took to the field with their weapons—Agnew used a Colt .45 service pistol—and "walked out through there killing the ones that were just wounded or hiding."

At one point they saw an injured German in a flooded ditch, only his head and shoulders above the water. His chest had been ripped open by machine-gun bullets.

"Give him a shot," said a chaplain who had caught up to them.

McNiece turned to Agnew. "You've got that forty-five," he said. "Blow his head off."

Agnew's first shot missed. Then he knelt, put the gunbarrel to the German's temple, and squeezed the trigger again, disintegrating his skull.

The chaplain was screaming at them. *"You know I didn't mean to shoot his head off! I meant to give him a shot of morphine!"*

"I'll tell you what, Chaplain," McNiece said, and looked at him. "You do anything you want to with your morphine. There will be a thousand paratroopers around here that will need a shot of morphine. We are not wasting it on these Krauts."

McNiece's response wouldn't have surprised anyone who knew him. He believed that if you were going to fight an enemy, you could never show or ask any mercy.

On the fifth night after the invasion, McNiece and the other men who'd fought at the Douve River Bridge reported to the 506th regimental headquarters, located eight miles west of Carentan, a German stronghold between Utah and Omaha Beaches. Beamesderfer would stay with the unit, joining the 3rd Battalion troops pushing to take the city. The Five-Oh-Deuce had tried, and then the Five-Oh-Ought, but the enemy had hung on. After that the Air Force bombers had hit the place hard, and now the 506th was going to make another attempt at seizing it.

The commander leading the group of four hundred or so men was Robert G. Cole, and he'd found the final causeway into the city obstructed by a heavy steel fence that the Germans were using as a barricade. As his men tried to get around it, one and two at a time, the well-hidden enemy soldiers in the hedgerows alongside the causeway would rake them with machine-gun and mortar fire, inflicting heavy casualties. Finally he ordered a frontal bayonet charge on the Germans through the hedges. McNiece had heard the Germans feared and hated bayonets after the close-in fighting of the First World War, and guessed that was why Cole decided to take them that way.

The charge got the Germans out of the hedges. But it cost more than half the battalion, and none of the survivors would ever forget how it felt to kill a man by thrusting a bayonet into his stomach—and know you would have been the one to die if you'd hesitated. Beamy would be very grateful for his Bible after that charge.

When they reached the city's outskirts where the bombers had struck, he and McNiece saw hundreds of dairy cows lying dead in the fields—cows and German soldiers, but almost no French civilians. Beamy wondered where all the people in those farms had gone. That was something that would always puzzle him, and when they got into the city, it was also like that. The streets were full of dead German soldiers, but the population had completely vanished.

Although the enemy had been mostly driven out by the fighter planes, it would take two days of door-to-door street fighting before they were completely routed. The troopers who'd marched into the city would hold it for another ten days before they were relieved, but the truth was the bombings hadn't left much of Carentan to hold. Its buildings had been pounded flat.

After the replacements arrived, McNiece, Beamesderfer, and the rest of the men who had taken Carentan were sent back to England for rest and resupply. Both men would see further combat throughout the remaining six months of the war—a great deal of it, in fact. But Beamesderfer's Pathfinder duty was at its end, while McNiece's was yet to come. And in a way that would make history.

5.

Captain Frank Lillyman's participation in the Allied invasion of France, and his role as lead combat officer of the 101st Pathfinders, ended on D-Day, when he was shot by a fleeing German soldier after coming to the aid of a threatened glider crew in a field behind Utah Beach.

The marking of the Keokuk landing zone would also be the final pathfinding mission of the Normandy campaign. There was to be no further need for parachute drops and airlifts as American and British forces continued to land on the beaches and establish themselves on the peninsula, and the volunteers of IX TCC Pathfinder Group would now fall in with their umbrella units—or, in the chaos of Normandy, other units—to help accomplish their regimental objectives.

The fighting at Normandy was bloody, and costly; an estimated five thousand Allied soldiers died on the Normandy beaches on D-Day alone. In the days before and after the invasion, about nineteen thousand French civilians were killed in bombings of enemy targets centered within population centers. The Germans, whose military records were left in disarray after the war—deliberately in many if not most cases—lost between four thousand and nine thousand men. But the fighting was so chaotic, and the loss of life so overwhelming in its proportions, that the actual casualty tallies on both sides were still being sorted out seven decades later.

For the Allies, Normandy was a decisive victory despite the heavy losses. Smashing through the Atlantic Wall, it dealt Hitler a blow from which he would never fully recover. By late June, more than three hundred thousand U.S. troops and an equal number of British infantrymen had come ashore on the Normandy beaches to begin their relentless push toward the French capital. On August 25, Paris was freed from Nazi occupation. The Third Reich was in retreat across Western Europe.

Shipped off to recover in a British hospital, Lillyman would skip out of the hospital, talk his way aboard a military supply ship sailing for France, and report for duty eight days after the invasion.

He would not, however, be cleared to return to combat until September, when he was reassigned to the 502's 3rd Battalion for the massive jump in the Netherlands that became known as Operation Market Garden. Later that year, he would lead a paratroop unit holding the snowbound town of Bastogne, Belgium, against a German siege meant to retake a portion of their formerly occupied ground and shatter Allied resolve. All told, Lillyman spent ten months in Europe fighting the war's most vicious battles, got wounded three times, and earned eight combat decorations.

Throughout his tour of duty, Lillyman would entertain himself by scribbling down notes about a dream vacation on which he'd take Jane and their three-year-old daughter, Susan, when he got home. After a while the idea took on reality in his mind and he began to save up for it. By the time he returned to his hometown of Skaneateles after the war, he'd socked away five hundred dollars for his imagined spree.

One night after a cognac or two, Lillyman, always a prodigious letter writer, sat down and dashed off a lighthearted wish list to the

Statler chain's Hotel Pennsylvania in midtown Manhattan, taking them up on their magazine ads claiming to provide extra special service for the families of war veterans interested in reservations.

I'd like a suite that will face east, and English-made tea that will be served to me in bed every morning, he wrote. *A phonograph with any and all Strauss selections. For breakfast, a fried egg with the yolk pink and the white firm, coffee brewed in the room so I can smell it cooking. The family breakfast should be served in the suite so we don't have to get dressed. No military title . . . "Mister" will be music to my ears. And there should be a large, grey-haired motherly maid for my daughter . . . a prodigious menu of such delicacies as filet mignon and lobster a la Newburg . . . a daily program of sightseeing, theatergoing and nightclubbing . . .*

Lillyman added several more items before ending his note with a provocative *Can you do it?* and then stuffing it into an envelope.

When the Lillymans arrived in New York City a few weeks later, a smiling hotel concierge told them that "everything was set" and their stay would be on the house. They were installed in a lavish five-room suite—"The George Rex!" the hotel boasted—with "an ashes-of-roses carpet, a sunken bathtub, a telephone rigged only for outgoing calls, and a buffet full of liquor."

In addition, *LIFE* magazine would report, the family was greeted with a bouquet of fresh flowers every day of the week . . . and everyone from the concierge and desk clerks to the bellhops and waiters called Frank "Mister." The periodical also mentioned that young Susan was so excited by the trip—and by suddenly having a personal maid at her service—that she forgot herself and ate her spinach.

Worlds away from the hell of battle, Frank Lillyman was getting plenty of attention for his valor and, unsurprisingly, not minding it a bit.

MARKET GARDEN

SEPTEMBER 17–25, 1944

Both fliers and airborne had been working as teams for almost six months, and nearly all were veterans of the Normandy drops. They knew their business and they knew each other.

—From the official U.S. military history of the operation

CHAPTER FOUR

1.

Word of the mission came down late for the Pathfinders. In fact, many were on weekend leave on Friday, September 15, only to have their escapades in the village watering hole cut short.

Technician Fifth Grade Glenn E. Braddock of the 101st Airborne was among them. Just recently off his recuperation furlough after Normandy, where he had jumped from the number two plane of Frank Lillyman's serial, the Kansas native had been having a "high old time" when he got the news.

Braddock was a tough, resilient sort of guy, a Golden Gloves boxer who rolled with the punches wherever and whenever they struck their blows—and it was no wonder. When he was four years old, he and his older brother Harry had been dropped off at an orphanage in Topeka by parents they would never know. The brothers were eventually adopted by the Daharsh family, but when

Mrs. Daharsh passed away at a young age, they'd found themselves back at the orphanage. Luckily, George Braddock, of Jewell County, needed hands to work on his farm and, mixing pragmatism and compassion toward a happy result, took them in and gave them his name.

A hard worker and quick study, Glenn had picked up a varied grab bag of hobbies in his twenty-five years on earth. He played guitar, banjo, and harmonica in whatever spare time he could find, and liked to sing a bit too—country music, mostly, learning the songs he'd heard the Carter Family perform on Border Radio, the five-hundred-megawatt broadcast dynamo out of Texas. The boxing was something he'd taken up in high school; back in the orphanage, he'd had to defend himself against some of the bigger, tougher kids who'd given him trouble, and that meant learning how to fight. The sport gave him a way to channel his aggressions and apply the skills he acquired with focus, endurance, and precision. At Camp Pike in Little Rock, Arkansas, where he'd gotten his basic training, Glenn won the lightweight boxing championship and wore the belt till his transfer to Fort Benning. As a T/5 in Pathfinder school later on, he'd been trained in how to use the Eureka box.

Operating the radar beacon was of course a serious responsibility. But Glenn Braddock held another job besides, a special role that set him apart from all others in the unit and showed the level of respect he'd earned from his peers and commanders alike.

An outfit's rigger was the soldier who packed and repaired the chutes. In the U.S. Army, his official motto was "I will be sure—always." It made total sense. Every trooper who jumped from a plane was entrusting him with his life. And a rigger had to value each life as if it were his own.

The job could be repetitive and mundane; perhaps for that reason, it required someone who was reliable, conscientious, and exactingly consistent, who above all else understood the words in his pledge that there could be "no compromise with perfection."

Braddock was honored to be that man for the 101's Pathfinders. Before Normandy, he'd packed, inspected, and personally signed off on all their parachutes in the marshaling area at North Witham. On the September night he learned of their second mission, it was Tom Walton, another veteran of the D Minus One drop, who broke the news to him at a Nottingham pub, letting him know there would be more packing ahead.

"We have to report back to base," he said, raising his voice over the music and laughter around them. "We've been designated for another possible jump."

Braddock had looked at him over his beer, trying to gauge his seriousness. But Tom's sober, earnest expression dispelled any thoughts that he might be pulling his leg.

A short while later, Braddock was in a jeep returning to North Witham. The troopers that Walton had rounded up would stop there briefly before they headed off to their new marshaling area at RAF Chalgrove, in Oxfordshire, about sixty miles closer to London.

The ride was a quiet one. They'd all experienced enough horror and destruction in Normandy for several lifetimes, and none would be gung-ho about heading into combat again. They had seen men killed and maimed, and some had barely escaped death or critical injury themselves. It had left irreversible marks on their souls.

As they bumped along over the foggy English roads, Braddock found himself wondering if this would prove the latest in a string of false starts they'd had since returning from Normandy. He wasn't alone among the men to hope for it, and with good reason. Just a month ago, a drop on Chartres, in northern France, to cut off German reinforcements had been scratched at the last minute, after Patton and his troops took control of the city. Two weeks later the Pathfinders had gotten their English currency exchanged for Belgian francs at the marshaling area, then been briefed about a jump near Tournai, a city hardly anyone had ever heard of. But a British armored division captured it in September, and the 101's planes had again stayed on the ground.

Ultimately, though, Braddock knew he had to push all that out of his mind. Whether his company returned to action wasn't for him to decide. His job was to get their parachutes packed.

At the marshaling area, he found things very different than they'd been before the D-Day jump, when the men had pretty well known what to expect. Yes, the invasion's exact location had been kept secret till a couple of weeks before it happened. And, yes, most of the Pathfinders had only learned its scheduled date around when they were ready to deploy. But they'd understood for months that they would be at the vanguard of the assault, and had a good idea they would be landing behind the lines in Occupied France. It had given them a chance to mentally, emotionally, and physically prepare.

Now they weren't told anything about the mission, or given any hint where they would drop. While the paratroopers were again under quarters and area arrest, there would be no long wait under heavy lockdown, no barbed wire fences, no armed MPs except at the supply room and Glenn Braddock's parachute shed. The little wooden structure would have some of the tightest security on base,

Colonel Joel Crouch. In civilian life, a United Airlines pilot. After Sicily, he brainstormed the Pathfinders idea with General "Jumping" James Gavin.

Captain Frank Lillyman chewing on one of his lucky cigars. When he ran low on his Army allotment, he had his wife mail him stogies.

Lieutenant Charles Faith and his stick pose before they board the C-47 for Operation Market Garden. Most will be killed when the plane is hit by German flak.

Officers, including Captain Frank Lillyman (center left),
look over a sandtable before the drop into Normandy.

The Rebecca unit (above) in the C-47 transport sent out a time radar pulse that was picked up by the Eureka (right), which the Pathfinders had set up in the drop zone. The Eureka sent back a confirming pulse to the Rebecca.

Sergeant Jake McNiece applies war paint to another trooper. He wasn't much of a garrison soldier, but he was a warrior on the battlefield.

Paratroopers drop on Holland on the first day of Operation Market Garden.

Troopers from the 101st make their way through the Dutch town of Veghel.

Jack Agnew sits on a pile of bricks in Bastogne. He will guard
the Eureka here for several days in the bitter cold.

with canine patrols constantly around except when he was inside working on the chutes.

On arrival at Chalgrove, Braddock learned he'd have fewer than half as many to pack than in early June. Just four sticks of 101st Pathfinders—each team consisting of an officer and nine enlisted men—had been moved to the marshaling area, compared to the eleven that had dropped into Normandy. It didn't mean the assignment was going to be any harder or easier than the last, but it did lead some of the troopers to conjecture it would be a day jump, since that would probably require fewer personnel and lights.

The men spent all day Saturday tossing guesses about the barracks. Most were friends from way back in paratroop school, and they did a lot of gabbing to relieve their anxiousness. Among them were the two scouts from Captain Frank Lillyman's Normandy stick, Fred Wilhelm and Bluford Williams; John Zamanakos, the demolition man; and the medic Snuffy Smith, his ankle having mended well enough for him to return to active combat status. Private Ernest "Dutch" Stene, who'd been in Braddock's stick in June, would be jumping again, as would his buddies Privates John Kleinfelder, Bill Mensch, and Corporal Roy Stephens.

They were a close-knit group, though some members of the Normandy teams were no longer with them. Gus Mangoni was now with Regimental S-2, and Zamanakos missed him. Lillyman himself had been transferred to a regular company command. A number of others also had been shuffled to other units. But with the exception of a single private, the officers and men awaiting orders at Chalgrove were old hands who'd done it before, and that was no coincidence. Because of the short window of time available for their preparation and briefing, the brass had sought experienced troopers for the operation.

That strongly declared preference had left the fresh replacements from the States out of the action despite being ready and able to contribute. The unit's commanders had spent weeks finding out which ones could cut it as Pathfinders and weeding out those who couldn't, forcing the entire company to repeat its specialized training course. The repetitive drills had irritated the old hands to no end. But their endless grousing about the "kids"—anyone who hadn't seen combat was called a kid, although they were about the same average age as the seasoned veterans—were really surface ripples on a deeper well of loss over the men who'd been killed or seriously injured in France.

No one felt this more than Braddock. He bundled their parachutes with his own two hands, inspecting the skin and ribs of the canopies, testing the links and lines, checking and rechecking the entire assemblies. Working late into Saturday night in his shed, carrying out his solitary responsibilities, he thought about the men whose chutes he wouldn't be packing and grew quietly sad.

Sunday morning came around fast for the Pathfinders. With few having gotten any sleep, they ate an early breakfast together in the mess. Steak and eggs, whole milk, fresh-baked bread . . . the hearty servings made them feel like they were being stuffed for the lion's den. At eight-thirty, they were called into a briefing, which in a sense bore out that suspicion. Told to prepare for their drop, they were issued their chutes, weapons, and supplies, and then informed they would be given their flight plan and orders at the airstrip.

Two hours later they were geared up and soaring over the English Channel. Their wait was over and so were the long hours of guessing. Like it or not, there had been no last-minute cancellation this time.

Their destination was Holland, where they would again be the first behind enemy lines.

2.

Three hundred and thirty-five miles away as the crow flies, Dutch resistance cells in and around the coastal villages of Veghel and Sint-Oedenrode had also gotten their instructions handed out on a strictly need-to-know basis.

Their superiors in the *Landelijke Knok Ploeg,* or Central Government Fighting Group, were perhaps even cagier than the big wheels of the 101st, and with good reason. The LKP's six or seven hundred members had been engaged in gathering intelligence on their occupiers, demolishing rail, telephone, and telegraph lines, and assassinating German soldiers and collaborators since their homeland's surrender to the Nazis in 1940. If they were caught as the result of any leaks or slipups, they would be killed as saboteurs, with the Germans exacting harsh retaliation against their family members, fellow townspeople, and anyone else believed to have lent them assistance. Their methods of reprisal ranged from sending suspects to prison, to deportation to concentration camps and merciless summary executions.

In Nijmegen, two members of the LKP, Johannes J. van Gorkum and Piet J. Jeuke, were at their headquarters in a shop near

FIRST TO JUMP

the city's main traffic circle when their commander, Sjef de Groot, contacted them over their backroom radio.

They were told to bicycle out to the heath at the edge of the Zonsche Forest by the Wilhelmina Canal and then "be alert and ready to help and provide information if necessary." Johannes was to identify himself as "Joe" and Piet as "Pete."

But to *whom*?

There had been no mention of that. The two young men weren't told who they were to meet or assist. They weren't told why they were being sent to the field. In fact, they weren't told anything about what was going on, except that de Groot and several others would be heading to a separate field north of their destination, outside the town of Eerde and southwest of Veghel. But they had their suspicions.

On Saturday afternoon, droves of American and British war planes had flown in over the fields to bomb and strafe railroad tracks, roads, overpasses, and German barracks and fortified artillery positions throughout the area. People in the city and nearby villages had taken cover at the roar of the Lancasters, Stirlings, Halifaxes, and B-26 Marauders. There had been reports over the underground radio that some of those planes had been downed by antiaircraft fire, but the Germans had suffered the worst of it.

Or perhaps that grievous distinction went to the Dutch people. The tiny village of Zeelst, outside Eindhoven, had been carpeted by Allied bombs probably meant for a nearby airfield. Dozens had been killed there and in other raids—men, women, and children. The carnage was beyond belief, and almost everyone held the German invaders responsible. They had grabbed civilian buildings for

152

their military use. They had built bunkers and gun emplacements close to homes and business. They had put the people in harm's way.

The Dutch wanted their freedom. But they had already lost much to the war and knew it was still possible to lose more. As they had secretly listened to news over the BBC of the Allied victories in France and Belgium, it had made them wonder if their country was next to be liberated. Many swung between fear and hope that it would be.

Johannes and Piet, barely into their twenties, knew those emotions could quite easily coexist in one's heart. As members of the LKP, they had placed their lives and the life of everyone they loved in jeopardy. But they had chosen not to accept their occupiers and in fact to take an active role against them. Pedaling out to the field that beautiful Sunday morning, the warm sunlight on their necks, they could sense something major was about to happen and brimmed with excitement over the possibility.

The nearby Wilhelmina Canal was above Highway 69, a narrow, two-lane asphalt-and-brick road running from Eindhoven to Arnhem. An important strategic corridor from a military perspective, it stretched from north to south above the surrounding fields, with four bridges branching off its shoulders to span canals and rivers on either side. If the Allies took the road and those bridges, they would be able to cross the Rhine into Germany and establish open lines of supply behind them.

Perhaps that was their plan, perhaps it wasn't. But the Germans had been observed digging foxholes near the bridges, which said a great deal about what they believed. Cycling out to Zonsche heath, the young freedom fighters could not help but feel they were on their way to welcome their American or British liberators. Why else would they have been told to become Joe and Pete?

It would not be long before they found out. They were speeding along on their cycles, Johannes a few yards behind Piet, when the sky began to throb with the sound of approaching aircraft. Within seconds, the noise grew deafening around them. Glancing up into the sunlight, they saw a German Messerschmitt tear through the air overhead, a British fighter in close pursuit. The planes were flying so low their markings were perfectly clear.

Then another plane appeared over the wide, flat horizon. This one wasn't a fighter, but a large transport. Awestruck, they saw a small handful men drop from its side as it passed over the Zonsche field, their parachutes blossoming open against the pale blue sky.

Scouts, Johannes thought. They were *scouts*.

Piet shot forward on his bicycle, leaning over the handlebars, streaking toward the heath where the paratroopers were coming down. Behind him, Johannes pumped his legs breathlessly but couldn't keep pace. With a quick glance over his shoulder, he realized he was riding past a field that belonged to a local farmer named Sanders, then saw him there watching and jumped off his seat.

Leaving the cycle with Farmer Sanders, he raced madly along the road to catch up with his comrade.

3.

Flying in serials of two, the four C-47 Dakotas of the IX Troop Carrier Command had taken wing with their sticks of Pathfinders at about ten-forty in the morning. The rest of the transports were scheduled to begin leaving England an hour later and continue their departures over the next four days. These flights would convey thirty thousand Allied paratroopers and glider-borne soldiers to the Netherlands, launching the largest airborne operation ever attempted.

Conceived by British field marshal Sir Bernard Montgomery, the plan was to bring a swift end to the war by having his infantry divisions cross the Rhine River at Arnhem and make a concentrated thrust into the heart of the Third Reich. It had originally met with resistance from SCAEF Eisenhower and General Omar Bradley, the commander of America's ground forces in Europe. After Normandy, they had arrived at a strategy of creating a broad front along the entire length of the Rhine, an overwhelming military force that would close in on the enemy's flanks like pincers as it advanced through German territory. Montgomery had vehemently differed with them. In his opinion, the invasion of France had left Hitler "weak on his pins," and it was time for a knockout punch. His stated objective was the industrial Ruhr Valley, but he was hoping to create a momentum that pushed straight on to Berlin.

A combination of political and military demands eventually led Eisenhower to warm to a limited version of Montgomery's plan, with the stipulation that it would have to fit within his overall broad-front strategy. Although he would rankle the British general by guaranteeing fewer supplies than requested, he agreed to commit all three U.S. airborne divisions to the attack.

The mission's airborne phase was codenamed Market; its ground assault, Garden. The combined operation, then, was called Market Garden.

Market's principal goal was to secure eight canal and river crossings along Highway 69 for Montgomery's Second Army. The 1st British Airborne Division and the Polish Parachute Brigade would make landfall at the northern end of the road to capture the bridges at Arnhem. The 101st Division's drop zones were slightly to the south, between Eindhoven and Veghel. The 82nd would jump still farther to the southeast and southwest of the corridor between the Rivers Maas and Waal.

As they'd flown across the Channel at an altitude of fifteen hundred feet, the 101's Pathfinder serials had been joined by a brawny Canadian P-47 Thunderbolt fighter escort. Its pilot would accompany the transports until they reached the coast of France, circling them repeatedly as he patrolled the air for hostile aircraft.

The escort had done nothing to allay the misgivings of Sergeant Marshall Copas. The twenty-two-year-old Kentuckian was pretty edgy, but a similar case of the willies had admittedly overtaken him when he'd dropped into Normandy. In fact, he'd been scared stiff. It hadn't helped that he'd thought he heard someone behind him after he landed. But when he'd whipped around, carbine in hand, he'd discovered it was only his chute—one of its lines had gotten caught on his canteen.

After about fifteen minutes Copas had settled down. He was trying to remember that, about as much as he would have liked to *forget* having gotten wounded later on by a German bullet fired from the hedgerows. But that night, at least, the Pathfinders had forty-five minutes to lay out their navigational aids. Now they would have twelve, about a quarter of that time. He and his buddy John Brandt also weren't encouraged by the knowledge that the "Tommies" were the ones coming to support them on the ground. Given their druthers, they later recalled, both would have wanted to see American soldiers. Taking it all together, was it any wonder Copas was nervous?

Up ahead in the Pathfinders' lead plane, Glenn Braddock had been a good deal calmer while gazing out a window at the Canadian fighter and his serial's number two transport. He was the cleanup man for his stick, one spot behind Sergeant John O'Shaughnessy and two behind the jumpmaster, Lieutenant Robert G. Smith, who'd been his parachute supply officer at Chalgrove. Smith and O'Shaughnessy had both dropped into the nightmarish inferno of Drop Zone D in Normandy, and they'd obviously managed to survive, so maybe they were lucky charms. On the other hand, Braddock didn't really like the cleanup position and had drawn straws with his buddy Roy Stephens, who'd just recently gotten a promotion from private to corporal, to see if they could swap flights. But he'd pulled the short straw and wound up in the lead plane. You won some, and you lost some.

Shortly after the Pathfinder serials turned overland toward Belgium, Braddock realized the Canadians had disappeared from sight. Stephens's flight, piloted by a lieutenant named Gene Shauvin, was close by, flying slightly behind and below his own transport.

"Don't you love me anymore?"

Braddock heard the voice over the intercom but wasn't positive which of the flyboys it belonged to . . . and a moment later he became too startled to worry about it. Shauvin had come up alongside his flight and gotten close, so close that Braddock would later insist the plane's wingtip poked through the open door of the troop compartment.

Christ! he thought. If the stunt had tickled his aircrew, it had just about made him jump out of his skin. For a second he'd been sure the planes would crash in midair.

Then Shauvin's plane dropped off a little. Apparently Shauvin was done hotdogging.

Braddock was watching him fall back into position when he heard the explosions, followed by "a rattle like heavy hail" on the roof of his transport. His eyes wide with horror, he saw smoke begin to pour from Shauvin's left engine and fuel tank. Then the plane nosed steeply down in that direction and hurtled toward the ground spewing flames.

Braddock stared out into the empty sky feeling walloped. He was a man who placed his confidence in diligent, careful attention to detail. In eliminating the element of chance wherever possible. But it was *pure* chance—the luck of the draw—that had spared him from flying aboard that transport instead of Stephens.

He wasn't certain how long it took for that to sink in. All he would remember later on was that he was still looking out the window when he saw the leading edge of his transport's wing turn into a gaping hole. A huge chunk had been blown out of it.

And it wasn't just the wing. Slugs were riddling the bottom of the plane, punching through the fuselage between the troop and the navigator's compartments. Braddock saw tracers with little tailing streamers of flame shoot up from the floor to the roof.

He looked around at the cabin, wishing he could take cover, hoping those rounds wouldn't drill straight through his seat into his backside. The navigator's door was closed. It had been open since they left England, but now he'd shut it. Sure he had, Braddock thought. Their plane was getting barraged with fire. Why would anyone leave it open?

"Flak tower to the left and firing at us!" someone shouted.

Braddock could no more tell who it was than he'd known who had been horsing around over the ship-to-ship before all hell broke loose. But the words turned his attention back to the window.

The tall, reinforced-concrete tower was visible rising from the field below, *to the left*, its 20mm guns chattering away from their turrets.

"Stand up, hook up, and check equipment!"

This time it was Lieutenant Smith, calling back over his shoulder. He wanted the troopers ready to jump as soon as the plane cleared the flak belt.

They hefted off their seats on his orders, laden with their packs and equipment. Standing, Braddock was a bundle of nerves—and he wasn't alone. The AA fire had continued pecking holes in the bottom of the transport, and the men wanted nothing more than to get past it.

He'd craned his head for another look at the enemy tower when everyone in the troop compartment heard the whine of a diving plane. It shrieked past them seemingly from out of nowhere, a British fighter, firing a stream of tracers at the flak tower—and then launching a pair of rockets from under its wing.

An instant later the tower went up in dust and smoke. Braddock joined an outpouring of cheers from the men around him as the ack-ack quieted, but that giddiness was short-lived. Their initial surge of relief quickly gave way to the awareness that they had lost a planeload of men. Their friends and brothers. It was a sobering moment.

But there was no time to dwell on what had just happened. Their transport had trimmed altitude. With the tower knocked out, its pilot, Lieutenant Centers, was descending for their jump.

They flew low for about five minutes. Then the transport climbed slightly, banking to the left.

"Red light, recheck hookup and equipment," Lieutenant Smith shouted.

Braddock carefully went through the checks before letting his eyes return to the window. In the field below were crisscrossing roads at the end of a long canal . . . and an old man and a little girl standing in the middle of everything. The girl was holding the man's hand with one of hers and waving up at the plane with the other.

Waving.

Braddock would never forget that.

Then the plane straightened out and the green light came on and he moved up the aisle to the jump door.

4.

Lieutenant Charles M. Faith, the squad leader and jumpmaster aboard Shauvin's plane, knew it had been struck by flak almost as it occurred. The Allied forces pushing in from Belgium had marked the front line with orange smoke for the transport pilots—orange was the banned national color of the occupied Netherlands—and it was soon after his flight crossed the line that the Germans had opened fire.

By that point Faith had noticed the ready light flashing above the door. Although the aircraft was about fourteen hundred feet in the air, twice as high as the optimal jump altitude, he'd ordered his men to stand up and hook up.

He was waiting at the front of the stick when the battery began raking the transport from below. Looking out a window, he'd seen the damage at a glance. Smoke was gushing from the juncture of the left wing and main fuel tank.

Faith could tell it was a bad hit, but he would have no time to absorb *how* bad before a massive explosion rocked the entire plane. As it took a hard tilt to the left and then seesawed downward, he went staggering to the open door.

The lieutenant would later come to believe that if he hadn't found himself right there in position to jump immediately, he'd have gone down with the aircraft. Standing at the door, hanging onto the frame, he had turned toward the front of the transport and seen a solid wall of fire between him and the pilot's cabin. It was like peering into a furnace.

He looked over his shoulder into the troop section. Weapons and supply bundles were skidding in the aisle as the transport swayed lopsidedly in the air. The soldiers packed together on either side had grabbed on to anything within reach, struggling not to fall under the weight of their gear. Lester Hunt, one of the enlisted men, was beside Faith in the number two position. Hunt, Mike Rofar, Ernie Robinson . . . he'd led them all into Normandy and handpicked them for his stick in today's mission.

But their goal now was just to survive. The plane was going down and they had to evacuate.

Faith didn't dare wait. He gave the go command, slapped Hunt's arm, then turned and bailed out the door.

The lieutenant plunged through space, his static line snapping taut as his canopy spread open above him. He heard the plane screaming through the sky and turned his head in time to watch its final moments. It hurtled earthward like a comet, trailing flames and smoke, then crashed into a field below with a terrific explosion, the fuel in its tanks igniting to envelop it in a gigantic fireball.

Faith knew he would never forget the image of the transport burning on the ground. He would see it vividly in his mind's eye until the day he died.

The seconds blurred by. As he made his descent, the lieutenant saw Hunt floating down to earth slightly below him—but no one else. Looking left and right, he still didn't see any of the others and concluded they mustn't have gotten to the jump door in time. More than a dozen men had been trapped inside the plane.

Faith held his risers tightly in his fists, trying to keep a firm grip on his emotions. As he neared the ground, he brought up his knees and prepared for his roll.

The soft, grassy field allowed for an easy landing. Standing up, Faith got out of his harness and Mae West vest and looked around. He saw no sign of Les Hunt. But there was a wooded area to one side of him, and he thought he'd heard some movement through the trees.

He slipped into the edge of the thicket and went toward the sounds, hoping they would lead him to the private.

They did, but not in the way Faith had expected. Parting the brush with his hands, he looked into another field and saw Hunt standing there with his arms raised in the air, a German infantryman steadying a bayoneted rifle on him.

Faith was still peering out between the branches when more sounds filtered through the greenery . . . but now they were coming from the field where he'd touched down.

He turned back in that direction to investigate, and what he saw made his whole body tense up. Another enemy soldier was standing over his discarded chute and harness, his weapon raised, looking edgily around for the man who'd been wearing it.

Faith watched for several minutes. He doubted two soldiers would go patrolling through these fields without backup. There likely would be more of them nearby. A squad, maybe an entire company. If he gave away his position, he would be captured like Hunt—or worse.

He backed deeper into the woods, trying not to make a sound. When he'd put some distance between himself and the field, he took off running at full speed.

Lieutenant Faith wasn't sure how far he ran before pausing to catch his breath. Then he heard German-speaking voices and ran some more, heading deep into the old growth forest.

After a while he stopped again, seeking out his bearings amid the tall Belgian elms and draping willows. Before their mission, the Pathfinders had received an intelligence briefing on escape and evasion, along with special double-sided maps printed on rayon fabric so they could be easily tucked away in their uniforms and wouldn't crinkle from wear, fall apart in bad weather, or rattle to alert the enemy when they were opened. Faith had kept the instructions from S-2 firmly in mind throughout his flight, using the E&E map and his wrist compass to move in a southerly direction.

He eventually found another way of orienting himself. The map showed an ancient stream, the Looiendse Nete, running north to south toward the French border—and he would pick up what he believed to be that waterway running its course through the woods and fields. Besides leading where he wanted to go, it provided freshwater for washing and refilling his canteen, and he resolutely kept its banks in sight as he journeyed on.

Finally he emerged from the woods, saw a hedgerow separating it from a roadway and field, and sprinted over to it, leaving the stream behind. The hedge wasn't nearly as tall or thick as those he'd seen in Normandy but was still bushy with summer growth. It would have to be good enough.

Exhausted, Faith plunged into the leaves and branches and hunkered down to rest.

He would spend the next five days there hiding from the enemy.

5.

"Hands up!"

Stopped cold in his tracks, Johannes van Gorkum raised his arms above his head almost before he'd realized it, holding them up straight as two flagpoles. He didn't need to see the Americans' weapons pointed at him to obey. But staring at their outthrust carbines and submachine guns, even at a distance of a hundred feet, did more than intimidate him. He suddenly found himself wishing he could return to the Sanders farm, hop onto his cycle, and pedal back to Nijmegen as fast as its two wheels could carry him. The soldiers had scared him to the core.

They approached without lowering their weapons, then patted him down.

"Let's go," said one of the men, finding him unarmed.

Johannes was ushered off the road and onto the heath, where he saw Piet talking to the Americans' commandant, his bicycle left on its side. Evidently his friend had already gained the officer's confidence. Realizing the two young Dutchmen were together, he had his troopers lower their guns.

Johannes—*"I am Joe!"* he'd repeatedly told the soldier who had walked him there—dropped his hands and listened. Piet spoke rapidly to the commandant, telling him about German troop locations in the area. The American paid close attention to the information, asked him a handful of questions, and then gave his men a brief set of orders. They immediately began to remove strange-looking equipment from their packs and duffels and lay it out on the field.

Unbeknownst to the Dutch resistance fighters, they had arrived at Drop Zone B/C, where the two planes composing the second Path-finder serial had deployed their troopers between Sint-Oedenrode and the village of Son. Lieutenant Gordon DeRamus was the leader of the squad that had jumped from Plane Number 3, and the man Piet was speaking to when Johannes caught up to him. Team Four's commander, Lieutenant Gordon Rothwell, stood within earshot near a drainage ditch, securing the area with his troopers.

This was the same Rothwell who'd headed the Pathfinder team that ditched into the English Channel on D-Day Minus One. Today he'd had better luck. His stick had landed on a dime almost side by side with DeRamus's men, the teams coming down so close to each other they hadn't needed to assemble. Together the two squads would prepare and guard a landing zone on a large field—actually several contiguous fields—that would be used by the 502nd Regiment's impending glider lift. Neither crew had any idea that Shauvin's number two plane had been shot down, and for Rothwell, fresh with memories of his own crash, it was probably for the best. He would need his full concentration for the job.

The ol' scarf was mostly the same as it had been for the Normandy landings: seven Holophane panels, colored smoke grenades, and a Eureka box. In addition, the Pathfinders would use an AN/CRN-4 glide path radio transmitter that could interface with a glider's onboard compass and had been rigorously tested at North Witham. The new portable beacon would allow for more accurate navigation by the glidermen—or so it was hoped.

Rothwell's men had primary responsibility for the electronic equipment, while DeRamus's group was to lay out the T with yellow marker panels—the letter "B" stenciled on them—and send up the smoke signals. It would be Fred Wilhelm who supervised the placement of the T, and John Zamanakos who set up and operated the radar equipment.

Their task completed without a hitch in four minutes, the Pathfinders at B/C were off to a quick start, an improvement over the delays and confusion that had characterized their Normandy misdrops.

But less confused did not necessarily mean less dangerous, as they would soon find out.

6.

Braddock felt muzzy and confused. His fingers were trembling as he tried to get out of his harness, a task made all the more difficult because the weight of his Eureka and other equipment had pushed him deeper into the straps. Still, it was giving him more trouble than it should have—if he knew his way around anything, it was a parachute rig. But he'd hit the top of a barbed wire fence when he fell to earth, and it had left him bruised and nicked up . . . besides sending him for a tumble that had knocked the stuffing out of him.

He blinked a few times, took some deep breaths to unscramble his senses, and fumbled with the hooks some more. Aside from

Dutch Stene, the rest of the stick at Drop Zone A had alighted on the other side of some trees, and he wanted to pull himself together and get over to them right away. Since he'd been the last man out of the plane, he figured he'd mentally line his position up with the drop pattern and retrace it . . . not a difficult thing with a clear head. But his brain still felt like mush after the rough landing.

"They're over here!" Stene yelled from several yards off.

Finally out of the harness, Braddock turned in his direction. He'd assumed Stene was talking about the men. But then he started shouting again—and this time he sounded alarmed.

"Hold it . . . there's someone spotted us," he warned. "Coming down the road toward us!"

His words raised Braddock's alertness with a jolt. He lifted his Thompson, thumbed off the safety for full auto fire, and waited.

A lone man in a pale blue military uniform was approaching him, walking along the edge of a ditch across the road. Braddock watched him closely, noticing he had a holstered pistol against his side. He steadied the tommy gun on him and waited.

The man did not slow down at all, but kept walking until he was directly opposite Braddock. He hadn't put his hand anywhere near his pistol.

"Take me to your commandant," he said.

Braddock looked at him over his gun barrel. "Ah," he said. "You speak English."

The man gave a nod. "Yes," he said. And then abruptly snapped up his hand.

It was a signal and Braddock knew it. But before he could react, two men in civilian clothes appeared out of the ditches on either side of the road. Both had rifles slung over their shoulders.

"I am with the Dutch Underground," the man said, offering his name as Sjef de Groot. "An officer."

In fact, de Groot was more than just an officer. His formal title was commander of the Brabant Regiment, and his authority covered the entire southern Netherlands. But he didn't give that information to Braddock, who wasn't about to relax his guard in any event.

He steadied the tommy gun. "Tell your men not to move or I'll kill you," he said.

Showing no desire to confront him, de Groot was calmly relaying the message in Dutch when another voice came through the tree line: "Where the hell's Braddock with the rest of the equipment?"

The T/5 didn't try to figure out which of the men that was. He had more pressing concerns—and getting his beacon over to the others was chief among them. The voice had reminded him that they had only minutes to set up the DZ before the main wave came roaring in.

"Stene . . . Stene, come over here quick," he hollered.

The private came trotting up on the double, his weapon at the ready.

Braddock motioned at the uniformed man. "This soldier claims to be a Dutch underground officer. But as far as I'm concerned he's still enemy," he said. "Take my equipment with him in front of you. If he makes a bad move, kill him. If I hear a shot, I'll start shooting likewise. If you hear a shot from this direction . . . let the rest of the stick know someone is with you. Or they might start shooting at you."

Stene nodded to show he understood.

"I'll stay here and act as security for the rest of the team, so they can take whatever precautions are necessary," Braddock said, thinking. Then he turned to de Groot. "Have you heard and understood what we have been talking about?"

"I understood."

"Okay, then," Braddock said. "Instruct your men to stay as they are until I walk out to the middle of the road."

The officer did as Braddock had ordered, speaking to his companions in Dutch. Then Stene moved behind him with his rifle and walked him and the transmitter equipment over to Smith.

The arrival of the underground men cut the timing closer than Braddock had realized. As he kept tense watch over them, wondering if they were who they claimed to be, the rest of the Pathfinders hurried to build the T behind the trees. It seemed to him that they'd no sooner gotten it done than he heard the thrum of the planes, saw smoke rise over the treetops from the DZ . . . and then saw the parachutes of the descending troopers fill the turquoise sky above.

As the troops floated down to earth, Braddock kept a suspicious eye—and ready Thompson—on the Dutchmen in spite of their cheers and applause at the men's arrival. Cautious man that he was, he would only lose his skepticism when Lieutenant Smith and de Groot came around a bend in the road, shaking hands with one of the paratroopers who'd made landfall.

More than two thousand men would jump into Drop Zone A as the 101st's forward parachute echelon was delivered to the fields north of Eindhoven, its transports homing in on the navigational aids set out by the Pathfinders. Down near Son at DZ B/C, Lieutenants DeRamus and Rothwell and their sticks would bring in more than four thousand additional 101st paratroopers, hundreds of equipment and supply bundles, and a lift of more than a hundred Wacos—the landings and drops carpeting four hundred acres of low-lying fields that spread out around the arriving sky soldiers as far as the eye could see.

In the words of a classified assessment written toward the end of 1944, the Screaming Eagle Pathfinders had accomplished their initial mission in Holland "efficiently due to excellent drops at slow speeds directly over previously selected pinpointed positions."

But the success of marking the September 17 drop zones had come at the cost of Lieutenant Gene Shauvin's flight—a price that would be dwarfed by the U.S. Airborne's overall losses as Market Garden skidded toward failure over the next seven days.

7.

Lieutenant Charles Gaudio and his copilot, Lester Vohs, had flown Plane 096 of the IX TCC on D-Day Minus One, dropping their squad of 82nd Airborne Pathfinders while under heavy fire from the ground. Now they'd brought in a stick from the 101st for the Holland jump—Lieutenant Rothwell's group—and had again pushed 096 through bands of heavy flak.

But Gaudio had learned a lesson from his first mission. As he'd made his pass over Normandy, the enemy gunners had shifted their aim toward the troopers, inflicting heavy casualties as they came down and preventing them from setting up their lights. Because he'd sped back across the Channel at once, Gaudio hadn't known the severity of the fire they were receiving on the ground and was quickly too far away to provide assistance.

He meant to avoid a repeat of that occurrence.

Approaching Drop Zone B/C, he and Vohs had been hit with small arms fire from some farmhouses in the middle of the immense clearing, and then spotted German gun and mortar teams outside the buildings. Determined to protect the Pathfinder teams as they installed their navigational aids, they'd looped back toward the farm and buzzed it, powering their aircraft low over its fields and rooftops.

It was a chancy maneuver for a plane without armaments, but Gaudio had bet on the Germans being caught off guard by the huge, noisy Dakota—and on the fact that they could have no sure knowledge it wasn't carrying a lethal surprise for them.

His tactic worked. The enemy guns had rattled up in his direction and been drawn away from the Pathfinders, who'd constructed their T in minutes. Looking down from his cockpit, Gaudio had seen the completed pattern of lights on the ground, veered away from the farm, and set a course for home.

At the DZ, the men had been grateful for the diversion. The Air Force had assured them nothing would move against them on the field, and with no sign of German infantry in their immediate area, they'd felt they could collectively inhale while awaiting the main body of paratroopers.

About twenty minutes after landing, Zamanakos, Wilhelm, and Snuffy Smith were standing watch by the T and talking when the shelling picked up again. There was a loud crash as a mortar round hit nearby and exploded into shrapnel.

Zamanakos felt a blast of warm air, then a hard clap on the side of his chest. The next thing he knew, he was down on the ground, his jump jacket and undershirt torn to shreds, the skin flapping off his exposed ribs where he'd been struck by a shell fragment.

He lay there in pain, his uniform filling with blood. Around him were Wilhelm, Smith, and Bluford Williams, who'd spotted a row of German tanks on a nearby road when they descended. They were about a quarter of a mile away, ten or twelve of them sitting under the roadside trees, and Williams would swear he'd seen their commanders drop down into their hatches during the jump. Although he was convinced they were hiding from Allied fighter planes, he thought they might have fired the rounds.

The men didn't know for sure. They were unaware of the enemy guns at the farmhouse, and hadn't seen movement from the tanks, so they could only venture guesses—and there really wasn't time for that. They had to get Zamanakos some cover while they guarded their lights.

It might have been Williams who suggested the drainage ditch running through the field near the T. Whoever's idea it was, they agreed it seemed like the safest place for the wounded trooper. Together a couple of them helped him to his feet and then got him down into the ditch.

Although the world kept swimming in and out of focus, Zamanakos never lost consciousness. Sitting with his back against the side of the ditch, his ribs on fire, he was aware of Smith crouching over him with his first aid kit, pulling out sulfa powder, gauze, bandages . . . whatever was available to patch up the wound.

The first of the 326th Airborne Medical Company's two glider loads arrived minutes later aboard six Wacos bearing vehicles, trailers, equipment, and more than fifty personnel who unloaded and set up an aid station at the southern end of the landing field. Zamanakos was brought to a ward tent, given further treatment, and eventually evacuated by ambulance to Son—liberated in the early hours of Market Garden—about twenty miles from the field. On that first day of Market Garden, the village's civilian hospital, the CBC Sanatorium, would be taken over by American forces and become the 101st's medical triage center.

Like many of those treated by the 326th AMC, Zamanakos was later moved to the 24th Evacuation Hospital in Belgium, and ultimately flown to England to recover.

Bombed, rocketed, suffering dozens of casualties, the 326th would remain operative for the next seventy-one days of combat in Holland, its doctors and nurses and medical technicians working tirelessly around the clock to treat thousands of wounded soldiers.

And to identify the dead.

CHAPTER FIVE

1.

In the late summer of 1944, with Hitler's Western Front pulling inward, the twelve-thousand-man Hermann Goering Training and Replacement Regiment in the Netherlands had braced for an Allied invasion. Established years earlier to train personnel for its parent unit, the Hermann Goering Parachute-Panzer Division, the regiment would, by September, be tasked with securing the southern part of the territory against a coastal and ground attack.

Its 3rd Battalion's five flak batteries were responsible for replenishing the HG P-P Division's ranks with antiaircraft and artillery gunners. One of these batteries—the *16 Flakbatterie*—was located at the Pont Fort heights outside the village of Retie, Belgium. With fears of an air attack mounting among German commanders, the position's inexperienced troops had been bolstered by veteran flak personnel from other units. This was the battery that had harassed the Pathfinders on their approach to the Market drop zones and that scored a lethal hit on Lieutenant Gene Shauvin's flight, IX TCC 981, over the dairy farm of Jan Adriaensen in the tiny rural hamlet of Kirtijnen.

Twenty seconds after going into its uncontrollable nosedive, the plane had come down in Adriaensen's garden and exploded in a sheet of flame, its burning debris hailing over the farmhouse. Half straw thatch and half tile, its roof instantly ignited. Within minutes the fire had consumed the house and barn, then leaped over to an adjacent barn belonging to a neighbor named Peer Franken.

Besides his wife Coleta and their three unmarried children, Adriaensen had been harboring his daughter Julia, her husband Jef, and their newborn baby Marie at the farm since the Allied air strikes began weeks before, his deep stone basement serving as a shelter during the repeated strafings and bombings. With the frequency of the raids escalating in recent days, the entire family had taken up full-time residence in the basement.

Shortly before the crash Jef, who'd been assisting with the chores, had gone out to the long wooden barn where his father-in-law kept his milk cows, pulled a fresh bale of straw off the pile with his muscular arms, then grabbed hold of a pitchfork and gotten to work. The bales were heavy and compacted, and separating the straw took effort. But he was glad to do it for the man who'd so generously opened his home to him in this time of extreme scarcity, when every morsel of food and bar of soap was precious.

He'd been spreading the straw across the floor when a tremendous *thump* stopped him cold with his hands around the pitchfork. Something had fallen to earth outside the barn, but at first he could only wonder what it might be. A bomb? It was possible. All he knew was that the object had been large enough for him to feel the impact underfoot.

Puzzled and alarmed, he dropped the pitchfork, rushed out the barn doors, and saw the wide pool of fire beside the farmhouse. Then he realized it had already spread to its rooftop and went running toward the house to get everyone out of the basement.

By the time Jan emerged into the daylight, his house and barn were ablaze. Sending his daughter Stan off to seek help from her brother Louis, whose farm was next door, he hurried across the yard with the other men to save his valuable livestock. They would try to set the cows loose before they burned to death.

Jan, Jef, and Louis couldn't get them out the barn doors, however. They were visibly panicked, tossing their heads and swishing their tails, their grunts and bellows awful to hear. But they had never been outside their stalls, and were refusing to budge, and the men didn't have any prods or sticks they could use to urge them on.

Still, they kept trying to get the animals out of the barn, doing everything they could to counter their nervous stubbornness. They slapped their sides and tried shoving them from their stalls, shouting, clapping their hands so they could be heard above the snapping roar of the fire, but it was of no use. With the fire climbing up to the rafters, and the heat and smoke inside the barn becoming unbearable, they wouldn't move. Finally the men had no choice except to abandon them to the fire. They ran out into the barnyard, coughing and gasping for air.

By now the farmhouse and Peer Franken's barn were seething with flames. Jan's family stood huddled together in the yard, watching the fire gnaw through the roof of his home, Coleta and the older children shocked and tearful, Julia's face a tight mask of anguish as she clutched her crying infant daughter to her breast.

They could hear the cows in the barn as they were incinerated. It made them want to cover their ears.

Jan Adriaensen felt as if he'd been struck by evil lightning. But he knew the tragedy could quickly expand beyond his personal catastrophe. Kirtijnen's six small farms stood within a half mile of each other, and almost everyone in the community had poured out into its country lanes after hearing the plane crash. Across the road, Adriaensen's neighbors had run from their home when the fire's baking heat had jumped through their windows, afraid of getting trapped inside if the conflagration spread—and their fear was far from unreasonable. Somehow, the villagers had to prevent the rest of their farms from going up in flames.

Hastening to fetch buckets and hoses, they banded together to wet down the other homes, drenching their rooftops and outer walls with water, praying that would be enough to impede the progress of the blaze.

Their cooperative action may have been why the fire didn't spread beyond the farmhouse and two adjacent barns. Watching it roar above the field, Adriaensen realized he'd been fortunate that his loved ones had escaped with their lives. But his home had been wholly consumed. He had lost his livelihood. Everything he'd owned was gone.

The farmhouse's skeletal embers were still smoldering when the Germans showed up to investigate the crash. A group of local Red Cross volunteers had also arrived to provide emergency medical treatment and aid in any rescue efforts, but their work would have to be conducted under the close scrutiny of the soldiers.

As they hunted through the scattered wreckage of the aircraft, they knew the odds of finding survivors were slim. If anyone aboard had lived through its impact with the ground, the flames that consumed it would have incinerated them.

The workers' grim expectations were confirmed when they discovered eight burned, mangled bodies outside a large section of the plane's fuselage. They would find the charred remains of a ninth man hanging from a seat on the left side of its cockpit.

Under directions from the Germans, the bodies were buried on the spot in eight graves along the side of the road. Fearing they would be accused of violating the Geneva protocols, the Germans would later order them dug up and moved to the cemetery in Retie. After the war, they were again exhumed, this time by the United States Army for permanent interment in the Ardennes American Cemetery and Memorial at Neuville-en-Condroz, in western Belgium.

All the Pathfinders and every member of the aircrew except for Gene Shauvin were positively identified. Shauvin was initially given MIA status, and then listed as killed in action, but aside from a mention in a Red Cross journal, there would be no official record mentioning the disposition of the remains seen in the cockpit, where he would have been situated before the crash. With eight graves for nine bodies, his family would come to believe that his remains were confused with someone else's and buried in the wrong coffin.

Of the contingent of Pathfinders aboard 981, the bodies recovered at the crash site and identified by their dog tags belonged to Privates George L. Sarlas and Michael Rofar, and to Corporals Roy L. Stephens and Delbert S. Brazzle. Not found were Privates

Earnest A. Robinson, Alvin Haux, Spencer E. Everly, and Lester R. Hunt; T/5 Richard H. Beaver; and their group leader, Lieutenant Charles M. Faith.

Faith, of course, knew Hunt had survived and been taken prisoner. Since he'd never seen their chutes in the air, he might have been surprised to learn that the four other troopers whose bodies weren't found had also survived and been captured by the Germans.

But at that point the lieutenant was just trying to stay alive and a free man. After roving more than a mile through woods, fields, and streams, he was tired and hungry and wondering how he would manage to stay out of sight until he made contact with friendly forces.

Concealed in his patch of shrubbery, he would wrestle with these questions through the long afternoon and night of his first day of hiding from the enemy.

2.

At Drop Zones B/C, the Pathfinder teams led by DeRamus and Rothwell were to stay out in the field for several days marking and guarding the DZs for glider lifts and resupply drops. But with no further landings scheduled in the smaller fields to the north, Headquarters had given Team A the assignment of helping the paratroops of the 501st PIR's 1st Battalion seize the town of Veghel and its four bridges—two spanning the River Aa in the village proper, and two south of it across the Willemsvaart Canal. Specifically, the Pathfinders were told to take and hold the bridge that ran into town across the River Aa, and to do it with all necessary haste. So great was the concern that the Germans would blow the crossings as they retreated, and eliminate them as rear supply lines for Montgomery's troops, that the goal was to have the bridges under the regiment's control by 1300 hours, or one o'clock in the afternoon, just half an hour after the Pathfinders touched down behind the lines.

The battalion's march from its drop zone had proceeded at a grueling clip. With their navigational beacon lost when Lieutenant Faith's flight was shot down, its forty-two sticks had been dropped at the wrong location, finding themselves around a spired medieval castle—Kasteel Heeswikj—in the village of Kameren, about six miles northwest of their intended DZ. The misdrops were remarkably concentrated, with all the paratroopers finding themselves within a short distance of the castle, and many coming down in its moat or surrounding trees.

There were relatively few casualties among the battalion's six hundred men, and those that occurred were accidental. From Kameren the paratroopers double-timed it to their objective without opposition, jogging sweatily in the warm sunlight under the arduous weight of their equipment. A few were given bicycles by the castle's caretaker and his companions, and would remember it as the first time they'd actually pedaled into battle. It was a peculiar feeling for them.

The Pathfinders and the battalion's forward element converged at the outskirts of Veghel to find themselves greeted by cheerful townspeople. They waved orange paper from doors and windows and poured from their tile-roofed homes onto the road, men, women, the old, and the young, all gathering around the Americans in their Sunday finest. There were boys in double-breasted red vests and baggy dress trousers, and pigtailed girls wearing white-winged caps, church dresses, and wooden clogs. They sang and danced with joy; they tossed flowers at the soldiers' feet and exchanged Dutch pounds for their invasion currency; they handed them bread, cheese, cake, apples, jugs of fresh milk, even ice cream.

As they neared the Aa River Bridge into the village proper, the troopers continued to be mobbed by civilians. A parade of children following behind him, one soldier felt a tug on his leg and saw a little boy with a red wagon pointing to his radio, trying to tell him he'd wheel it into town. Since the radio had been damaged in the jump, the trooper agreed and took it off his back. He would recall thinking the boy seemed "about the happiest little Dutch boy in the entire country. You could see the pride in his face."

The exuberant reception gave the soldiers a much-needed boost. For a short time it seemed to suspend the war and simultaneously remind them why they were fighting it. It was a recollection many would later reference, something that would sustain and replenish their morale in the dark days to come.

The small group of Pathfinders split up at the bridge. Per his orders, Lieutenant Robert Smith stayed behind to hold the span with four of the men, while Sergeant John O'Shaughnessy, T/5 Glenn Braddock, and the rest of the team joined the 501's forward element moving on along the Willemsvaart Canal into Veghel. Their task was to clear the village streets and establish a blockade at the market square's main intersection.

Before their departure at Chalgrove, the troopers had received mimeographed translation sheets from S-2 with basic Dutch phrases on them, and they'd folded the slips of paper into their pockets or under their helmets as they boarded their planes. They proved more than handy. Walking off the bridge, O'Shaughnessy, Braddock, and the others used the phrases to ask the locals to guide them to the square and point out possible German hiding places.

The canal dead-ended at the intersection, where the soldiers found a camouflaged gun nest. After a quick inspection revealed it to be unoccupied and strewn with rubbish, they hastened to set up their roadblock.

Braddock would remember that they'd barely gotten started when someone shouted, "There's Krauts running into that building on the left!"

He and Sergeant O'Shaughnessy looked around, saw a group of Germans running toward a long brick building across the square, and took off in heated pursuit, several other troopers following them from the gun emplacement. But the enemy soldiers had gotten a head start and already reached the house. They bolted in different directions, most racing through the front door, the rest fleeing around behind the building.

Close on their heels, Braddock and O'Shaughnessy ran straight up to the door, the other troopers staying with the Germans who'd gone around back. As the door practically slammed shut in O'Shaughnessy's face, he kicked it open and threw in a hand grenade.

There was a loud explosion inside the place. Braddock, also fisting a grenade, was about to pull the pin, but the sergeant had charged inside with his Thompson ablaze. Braddock hurried after him through the door, his own sub raised in his hands.

They were on the ground floor of an industrial warehouse, the room around them cavernous in its dimensions, an open door on its opposite side. Both men knew at once the Germans must have fled through it.

Their footsteps echoing flatly off the walls, the Pathfinders ran across the room toward the doorway, and were about to enter it when they heard heavy fire outside. Braddock stopped and peered through.

Three Germans lay dead on the ground, their uniforms riddled with bullets, blood flowing from their wounds into the spaces between the cobblestones. A lieutenant and several of the others who'd swung around behind the building had shot them as they emerged, then moved on up the street. Glancing in that direction, Braddock saw the bodies of two more German soldiers.

The lieutenant's name was O'Connell, and he was new to combat. Jumping over the bodies of the Germans, he had thought, *Thirty seconds ago they were alive.*

Thirty seconds.

That was the moment the reality of the war came to him. A man had to be ready to kill, and ready to die, and the difference between one fate and the other could be as simple as deciding whether or not to step through a doorway, or turning right or left. O'Connell knew it could have easily been him on the cobbled ground, and a German soldier glancing down at his body as he ran past. Could have been his mother, and not the mother of one of the men whose lives he'd ended, who soon would be mourning the loss of a son. In a strange way, the realization formed an inseparable link between him and the enemy, an awareness of how much the same they really were under their uniforms. *Soldiers.* Their lives were all hanging on slender threads, and they controlled far less about how and when those threads would be cut than any of them might have chosen to believe.

Standing in the doorway, Glenn Braddock could not have known the lieutenant's thoughts. But he would avoid looking too closely at the bodies before he turned from the doorway into the warehouse and then walked back out and across the street to the end of the canal.

3.

Not far from the warehouse, toward the center of the square, the townspeople skipped, bobbed, and held hands doing their circle dances, while the village priest stood passing out beer and pretzels in the courtyard of the old gothic church. Smiling and joking amid the hoopla, he resembled a pudgy, cheerful penguin in his black-and-white vestments.

Back at the gun emplacement with the 1st Battalion men, Braddock would recall the sudden clanking sound—and then one of the troopers commenting on it as they worked to set up the roadblock. He thought it was a British tank, and so did several of his companions. They'd heard Montgomery had broken through the enemy lines, and figured his armored forces had come right on time to provide them with support.

Then another soldier's voice cut in, its tone very different than the first.

"It's a Kraut light tank!"

The troopers were all looking into the square now. The treaded vehicle barreling toward them had an Iron Cross painted in front, and a man in a black officer's cap standing up out of the turret with a German Luger.

Braddock heard somebody call for a bazooka team, and then remembered passing one on the way from the bridge. He was starting back there at a fast clip when the Panzer's machine gunners opened fire, their long, rattling volleys followed by the heavy boom of the Panzer's cannon. Then came the answering sound of American rifles and submachine guns.

Braddock would always believe the officer spotted him right before ducking down into the hatch. Possibly he took him for one of the soldiers firing at the tank and got angry. Whatever the reason, it was then that that the Panzer turned in his direction, rolling straight at him, its huge steel gears making a tremendous clamor in the square.

Only a short while after Braddock had chased the group of doomed Germans into the warehouse, the tables had turned. He'd become the pursued, and was running for dear life.

Reaching a corner building, he hooked around into the street behind it, thinking he could make for the opposite corner and dash out of sight. Instead, he found himself staring at a high rock wall or fence behind the house. He had no idea what it was doing there but knew he couldn't get through. He'd been cut off from the other side of the street.

Braddock was trying to decide what to do when he heard the clanking of the armored machine's gears again. Turning, he saw that it had swung into the backstreet and was rumbling closer.

He looked desperately around, realized he was standing outside a door, and kicked it open. As he barreled through, he heard the cannon boom a second time, pulverizing a section of the building's exterior.

Then he was inside the house. There was an entry to another room in front of him, two women and a small boy huddled tight against the opposite wall. He waved a hand to let them know he meant no harm, paused in the middle of the room, and listened.

The tank seemed to be drawing away from him. Listening some more, he grew convinced of it. The gunner had backed off.

Although Braddock could not see it from inside the house, the tank had returned to the corner and made a sharp right into the square, plowing through the gathered townsfolk, scattering them in all directions.

As it tore through the intersection, Sergeant O'Shaughnessy drew his Colt .45 and took off after it, pumping rounds between its chassis and turret, aiming for the soft spot he'd been told about in basic training. At the same time another soldier was vainly attempting to jam his M1 rifle between the tread and the wheels. But the vehicle roared toward the bridge, its machine gun spraying the intersection. Miraculously, not a single person was hit.

The troopers were still firing away at the tank when Braddock left the house where he'd taken cover. He stood in the square and saw the Panzer vanish down the road, bearing out of town. As quickly as it had appeared, it was gone.

The square was quiet, but not for long. As American troopers continued marching in over the canal and river bridges, the gaiety began to build. Soon the dancers were again skipping and bobbing across the cobblestones outside the church, post office, and town hall.

As he looked around the square, Braddock would have seen the 326th engineers arriving to construct their secondary bridges for the armor and trucks heading on to Arnhem. But first the town's entry and exit points had to be secured.

Crossing the square, he went to the intersection, joined the men at the abandoned German gun emplacement, and got back to work.

4.

Two days after landing at their DZ, the Pathfinders of Team B/C continued marking the drop zones for gliders and supplies. On September 18, Colonel Joel Crouch had decided that Rothwell and DeRamus would themselves require an immediate resupply of essential items. "Due to the weight and bulk of navigational aids," a top secret report stated, "it was impossible for them to carry in enough smoke and batteries to provide continuous operation of all aids for subsequent landing of gliders."

The resupply was to consist of a complete CRN-4, extra batteries for it and the Eureka set, plus additional smoke.

Lieutenant Al Burckhardt, in IX TCC's Plane 086, made the successful drop, and the equipment landed within twenty yards of the Eureka on which his aircraft homed in.

On the ground, the Pathfinders were growing tired and frayed. Bluford Williams had repeatedly found his mind going back to the dozen or so German tanks he'd seen lined up under the trees along the road. Whether or not it had been one of their cannons that struck down Zamanakos, he'd never seen them pull out and couldn't stop imagining what would happen if they left the highway and came rolling across the field, their guns turned on the two sticks of Pathfinders.

Think what damage they could do, an inner voice kept repeating. *Think what they could do.*

Although these thoughts continued to trouble Williams as he guarded the T, Allied fighter planes had annihilated or driven off most of the Panzers lurking in the area. The fighters had roared down over the treetops, hitting them with bombs and machine-gun fire while they sought concealment in fruit orchards or tried to rumble off across the fields.

For the residents of nearby villages, the aerial pursuit of the Germans was a harrowing experience. The Allied planes came circling in low over homes, schools, hospitals, and church steeples, hunting out enemy tanks and cars, spraying anything that moved with bullets, and dropping racks of bombs on the streets and gardens. Explosions rocked the walls and sent dust cascading down over huddled, fearful men, women, and children in the underground shelters where they'd taken cover from the strikes.

At the drop and landing zones, the Pathfinders were finding out that the Army had held to its pledge—nothing on the ground had been allowed to move against them while they set up and guarded their equipment. Exposed and vulnerable in the open field, they had known their lives depended on that promise being kept. More importantly, they'd needed to *trust* it would be kept. They would guard the T with their lives, and their leaders would do everything to protect them while they stood their ground. It was more than an assurance to the men. It was a bond of honor that would allow them to move past their fears and carry on despite the unforgettable horrors they were to witness.

In the first hour of the landing, they'd seen about seventeen C-47s shot down in the fields around them, so many that it had made DeRamus suspect the Germans had gotten advance word of the drop. Johannes van Gorkum, the Dutch freedom fighter, noticed the cannonades coming from the direction of Best to the south, and informed the Americans about the placement of Nazi troops in the village and neighboring Son.

But Gorkum's intelligence, if ultimately used, had been received too late to cut those early losses. Some of the wounded planes had come on hard and fast above the ground like blazing comets, several with troopers hanging from their wings. One transport with flames sprouting from its engines had plowed out of control through a stick of paratroopers as they hung suspended from their canopies, killing at least two of them before it crashed. Williams would remember watching several transports swoop down no more than fifty feet above the Pathfinders' heads and wondering if their pilots were dead, if they were being flown in by their copilots or crew chiefs, or if there was anyone at all alive in the cockpit to man their controls. Barreling though the sky at that altitude, the soldiers aboard those damaged transports had been left with no time for their chutes to open in the air, and probably no time to hook up their static lines. But they'd leaped from the planes in futile attempts to evacuate and fallen to their certain deaths, hitting the ground like rag dolls, their bodies left shattered and bloody on the field.

Williams would always recall the image of one badly wounded glider transport that had flown burning over the DZ, losing altitude at first, and then veering upward in a steep, sudden climb with the glider still in tow. His neck craned backward, shielding his eyes with his hand, he'd watched it soar up and up and up like a fiery arrow, *straight* up, shooting a half mile into the sky, or what seemed a half mile, dragging the Waco behind it by its cable, the two aircraft dwindling in Williams's vision until they seemed no larger than scale models, then reaching the peak of their ascent and exploding before his dumbfounded eyes.

As the Pathfinders steadfastly followed procedure and guided in the planes, Snuffy Smith would feel an identical, lasting sorrow over the men that were shot out of the air. In Normandy, they'd seen planes and gliders downed by antiaircraft batteries. But in the skies over Holland, Luftwaffe fighters would defy the Allied escorts buzzing over the unarmed C-46 transports and sweep in to pick them off like predatory hawks.

The vicious dogfights between the warplanes were sights Smith would never be able to purge from his memory. For someone who'd always felt a calling to alleviate human pain and suffering, it was terrible to stand by and watch the battles overhead, knowing there was nothing he could do to help the men in the air. At the time, Smith was convinced that he would never experience anything that made him feel more hollow and impotent than those awful moments during Market Garden.

Four months later, outside the Belgian village of Bastogne, he would find out he was wrong.

5.

Almost five days after he'd bailed out of his burning transport, Lieutenant Charles Faith was wearing down. He'd spent most of that time in the evergreen hedge, leaving it only under cover of darkness to fill his canteen in the stream, attend to his bodily functions, and work the stiffness out of his neck and limbs. But he was simultaneously hungry and suffering from intestinal cramps and diarrhea—none of which surprised him.

Because of their heavy bulk and weight load, the Pathfinders had not been given the field rations normally issued to airborne troopers. Instead they'd jumped with only their emergency G rations—military chocolate—and eating them had sent the lieutenant's bowels into an uproar. Produced by the Hershey's company, the hard, bitter bars were intentionally unpalatable to discourage soldiers from consuming them as snacks. But the men had also found the high-energy chocolate indigestible and murder on the teeth, and it was no wonder that they'd dubbed it "Hitler's Secret Weapon."

Going through one a day, Faith had already used up all five of his bars . . . and while it was difficult to lament their absence, they'd at least been crude sources of nourishment. Now he could feel himself starting to fade from hunger and exhaustion. He craved real food, something that wouldn't turn his stomach and give him the runs. The hedge where he'd spent the last five days had been a lifesaver. But he needed to move on.

He would never know whether to call it chance or a godsend that he heard the slow clomp of hooves and the creak of wooden wheels on the other side of the bushes. Peering through to the bordering lane, he saw a man in simple farm clothes riding toward him in a horse-drawn cart.

Faith's heart raced. This was his opportunity. As the big workhorse drew closer, Faith rose from his crouch and stepped out of the hedge into the middle of the lane, leaving his Thompson on his shoulder to demonstrate he meant no harm.

The man in the carriage sat up in his seat, checking the horse's reins with an easy tug to halt several feet up the road. He stared at Faith across the lane, his features guarded.

Faith looked back at him. Filthy, unshaven, and stinking of sweat, he realized he was anything but a pleasant sight. But he'd hung on to the sheet of paper he'd been given with the collection of phonetic Dutch phrases on it, and figured there was no time like the present to see how useful it could be.

"*Goedendag,*" he said. "*Ik ben een Amerikaanse soldaat.* My name . . . *mijn naam* . . . is Charles Faith. *Kunt u me helpen?*"

And then he waited.

The farmer eyed him for a long moment. Then he nodded as if in response to his own silent question. He'd made his decision.

In broken English, he introduced himself as Fox Gust. Faith had wandered into his farm, in the village of Duinberg, he explained . . . and if he chose, he could come home to stay with his family. The British were pushing down from Antwerp, which had been liberated about two weeks earlier, and it was said they had been making fast progress. There was room for Faith to sleep in the basement of the farmhouse until they arrived and secured his village. The Gusts had food, and water, and civilian clothes he could wear while hidden there.

Faith didn't hesitate. With a broad smile, he climbed into the wagon beside Gust and extended a grubby hand. A minute later, the horse was clomping up the lane again, both men riding behind it with the late September sun on their shoulders.

The lieutenant would stay with the farmer about a week before Allied troops—Canadians and Scottish armored brigades, as it turned out—came rolling into the village aboard their jeeps and tanks. When Duinberg's liberation was officially declared, Farmer Gust and his brood would ride Faith into the village aboard the same wagon Gust had used to bring him home. There before the town hall, a traditional *harmoniemuziek* band in red vests and white-and-black trousers greeted him with an exultant fanfare, their woodwinds and horns blaring, their drums, cymbals, and bells clattering zestily away.

Lieutenant Faith would not jump again. But Joel Crouch's IX TCC Pathfinders had one final mission ahead of them—and the fortunes of the Allied campaign in Europe would hinge on its success.

6.

Operation Market Garden was several contradictory things at once. In its worst aspects, it was a strategic, tactical, and logistical blunder of terrible magnitude; in its best, a triumph of courage, persistence, determination, and sheer fighting skill for the two United States airborne divisions, who landed with near-pinpoint accuracy at the drop zones and landing zones established and protected by the IX TCC Pathfinders.

On September 22, five days after Pathfinders guided in the first massive paratrooper and glider drops, the German Army's 107th Panzer Brigade moved in from rear positions where they had camped based on prior intelligence, to cut Highway 69—Hell's Highway, as it came to be called—north of Veghel and south of Arnhem and Eindhoven. The successful armored thrust blocked vital supplies from reaching the 1st British Airborne Division and the Second Army's XXX Corps at the Arnhem crossings and, after inflicting heavy casualties, eventually led to their withdrawal. The bridge across the Rhine was never attained, and Montgomery's desired knockout blow never struck. Instead, his forces were left on the ropes to try and regroup.

The bloody turn of events at Veghel encapsulated the overall situation as it would develop. The 502nd PIR's taking of the village, the rousting of its German overseers, and the celebratory welcome the paratroopers received from of the Dutch populace was a triumphant, almost euphoric occasion. But within days Veghel was under siege by German armor and infantry, and while the 502's troops, with the aid of reinforcements, held on to repulse the attackers, the losses they took need never have been suffered.

There would be considerable debate about the reasons Market Garden was undertaken in the first place. Some would attribute it to overconfidence on the part of the Allies, and Montgomery in particular. Others would blame politics, at least in part. The combining of all Allied paratroop divisions in America and Europe into the First Allied Airborne Army had occurred at the order of SCAEF Eisenhower in early August, and it was argued that he'd felt pressure to launch a major airborne operation that would show America's elected leaders, eager to make rapid progress in the war, the capabilities of this pooled force.

Market did hasten the liberation of Holland and other parts of the Netherlands, and in that regard achieved a degree of success—although Allied forces advancing from the southwest were already well on their way to attaining that goal, and would have done so in relatively short order at a much lower cost in lives and material resources. But it is possible that the operation's real military payoff for the Allies, and specifically its airborne units, might have come months after it was aborted, and was therefore overlooked:

Whereas Normandy had been all disorder and confusion for the paratroopers of the 101st and 82nd Airborne Divisions, Holland showed them what they could do when their deployment was properly and accurately executed and their teams could assemble as planned. The broader mission might have failed, but they did everything that had been expected of them. And they knew it to a man.

Ultimately Market added a sense of unit cohesion to the U.S. airborne infantry's existing confidence as soldiers, and in doing so forged them into an improved fighting force. The men came out of Market Garden tougher, stronger, and more resilient than they'd been when they came in.

Two months later, in Bastogne, Belgium, when they had little besides those qualities to sustain them, it would make all the difference.

THE SIEGE OF BASTOGNE

DECEMBER 20–27, 1944

I was the biggest goofball the Army ever saw. The Lord only had two places to put people, Heaven or Hell, and He was afraid to stick me in either one, figuring I'd goof it up.

—101st Airborne Pathfinder Jake McNiece

CHAPTER SIX

1.

After seventy-eight days of combat and a week of being absent without leave, Jake McNiece had returned to base camp in Mourmelon, France, feeling bone weary. He'd figured the AWOL had been a fair reward for all the killing of Germans he'd done in Market Garden, but the Army showed its disagreement by putting him under arrest in quarters the minute he got back. That meant he would be restricted to the barracks and have his pay docked and possibly find himself knocked down in rank for the third or fourth time.

Jake's pal Frank "Shorty" Milhan was in charge of quarters, the noncom who handled the administrative thisses and thats for the higher-ups during the overnight hours. He also played watchdog over the entrance to the barracks. Built by Napoleon in the 1850s, the stone huts were being used by the 101st after their return from the Netherlands. The division had lost about 40 percent of its men and was filling its ranks with replacements who'd made the place pretty crowded.

Mourmelon was a little town with about ten bars and maybe a dozen whorehouses, and McNiece had felt he deserved better than to have to wait in line behind some green recruits for the drinks and girls. So he had gone off to Paris a couple of days after Thanksgiving, bumming rides for about ninety miles on the A4 motorway.

He'd had a fine time there in Paris.

"Jake, how would you like to go to England?"

This was Shorty talking now. He'd followed McNiece from the gate and caught up with him the minute he dropped his gear bag onto his bunk.

McNiece looked at him. "Oh, is England where they're going to hang me?" McNiece said. "I don't like them French guillotines."

"That's not exactly it, Jake," Shorty said, and hesitated. "It's almost. They would like you to volunteer for parachute pathfinding service."

Pathfinding service. McNiece guessed this was the sincere thanks the Army was giving him for Holland. His demolition stick had jumped over the country with the rest of the Screaming Eagles on September 17 and drawn the initial mission of taking the three bridges at Eindhoven. The Germans had wired them to blow so the British troops could not advance toward Arnhem and cross the Rhine, and McNiece's team had successfully dismantled the explosives and held the bridges.

The German counterattack on the second day of Market Garden had been punishing. Four Messerschmitts had swooped in over the canal and bombed the bridges. The bombs had taken one of them out and killed or injured quite a few troopers. Then a few days later, McNiece and his group had been ordered up to Veghel to join the British troops who were holding the town after it had been taken by the 101st. The battered troopers had driven there in an abandoned enemy truck and encountered no resistance on the highway. But when they reached the market square in Veghel, they started taking small arms and mortar fire from all sides.

That had been a hard way to learn that the Nazis had recaptured the town from the Brits. Its buildings were infested with enemy soldiers, and the bloody, door-to-door fighting had been without letup until the Americans finally pushed the Germans out.

Things had gone on like that without letup through the end of October and into November. Then the demo-sabos had been on risky minefield-clearing duty right through Thanksgiving.

McNiece had lost all but four of his teammates in Holland. He was sick and tired of the Army. And he guessed the Army was sick and tired of him. From what he knew of Pathfinder duty, it was "like volunteering to kill yourself."

Captain Gene Brown and Lieutenant Schrable Williams were the top dogs in McNiece's outfit, and though he got along with both of them, Williams had always had his back. Figuring Brown had given in to pressure from above to clean house of troublemakers, McNiece reported straight to his office.

"What happened to all those guys who volunteered for this Pathfinder bullshit in Holland?" he asked, saluting.

"They came back and unvolunteered," Brown replied.

McNiece had a good idea why. In Holland, the troopers had seen it as a way to get pulled out of combat. But here in the heart of champagne country, watching new American movies once a week, they were no longer so eager to take a training that could plunge them right back into battle—on suicide missions, no less.

Except, McNiece told himself, maybe those guys hadn't thought it out well enough. Maybe there was something to the offer that would make it worthwhile. Something they hadn't seen at first blush.

Looking at him across his desk, Brown, perhaps unsure how to interpret his silence, was already sweetening the deal. "If you volunteer, you'll leave the Five-Oh-Six with a clean record," he said. "And retain your rank."

McNiece wasn't tempted by these inducements. He had never cared about his record, or how many chevrons he wore on his arm. Still, he wanted to consider the whole thing.

Promising Brown he'd have an answer in an hour, he left the office and mulled it all over. Hitler was almost cooked. The Americans and British controlled the air and sea and had liberated most of Western Europe. Meanwhile, the Soviet Army had rolled through the East and marched across the German border in October. What would lead to another massive paratrooper jump of the type that required Pathfinders?

McNiece examined the question up, down, and sideways in his mind and didn't see how they would be needed. The Army pencil pushers might see it differently, but he figured he would go ahead and accept the offer. It would be his ticket out of the war. Not only that, he'd spend its remaining months at Chalgrove eating good Air Force food instead of Army slop.

"Yeah, I'll go," he told Brown back at his office. "I'm packing now."

The captain looked pleased. And why not? thought McNiece. He was finally getting him out of his hair. He was also probably thinking he was as good as dead, but that was no longer Brown's problem.

For his part, McNiece was also happy. He'd already imagined himself making out with pretty, attention-starved Oxford University girls—call it postgraduate work—while their boyfriends were somewhere across the Channel taking on the Third Reich.

"One thing," he said. "You've got to take me off arrest of quarters here. I want to go around and say good-bye to a bunch of these guys and thank them for the way they served."

Brown didn't have a problem with it, just so long as McNiece was ready to leave in the morning. Then he got a look like the cat eyeing the goldfish bowl. "What about Majewski?" he asked. "Will Majewski go with you?"

McNiece stared at him. Max Majewski was one of the original members of the Filthy Thirteen. A big, blond-haired, blue-eyed lug that some guys thought was a little slow upstairs but who was smarter than most of them, and as steady a man as anyone McNiece had ever commanded.

Majewski had earned a combat award called the infantryman's badge back in Normandy but then had it taken away from him. How that happened was he'd gone on leave back in England and come back with a venereal disease, and their commanding officer had reprimanded him by quashing his receipt of the award.

Thinking it unfair punishment, Majewski had written a letter to a column in *Stars and Stripes* called the "B-Bag." In infantryman's parlance, that was short for barracks bag. There was an expression that went "blow it out your b-bag" for when a soldier griped about one thing or another and his buddies felt he'd gone on long enough, and an editor had gotten the idea to use it as the title for his complaints column. If he felt a soldier's claim merited action, this editor would bring it to the attention of an appropriate party—and that party was often General Dwight D. Eisenhower.

As it turned out, Majewski's letter was one of those that had wound up in the SCAEF's hands, and from what McNiece had heard, Ike had gotten angry and personally given hell to the entire chain of command. "They really took a lot of heat for it," he remembered, "from the top man down to the bottom man." And they'd carried a grudge. In McNiece's view, the captain wouldn't have at all minded sending Majewski off on an assignment that would get him killed.

"Wait a minute,"he said. "I'm not encouraging Majewski or anyone else to go into Pathfinding service. That's your problem. You talk to him."

Brown must not have wasted an instant doing it. A half hour later, McNiece was back at the barracks, appropriately enough packing his b-bag for the transfer to England when Majewski came in.

"Jake," he said, looking at the bag, "what are you doing?"

"I'm packing my stuff."

"I thought you were under arrest in quarters," Majewski said. He seemed confused. "I didn't know you had privileges to travel."

"Yeah, I have," McNiece said. "There'll be a plane here in the morning to kick me out."

"Well, Captain Brown called me in and said he'd like me to go with you," Majewski said. "What made you decide this was a good move?"

McNiece explained why he figured there would no longer be any large paratrooper drops, and how going to the Pathfinder

THE SIEGE OF BASTOGNE

school would be a choice way to sit out the rest of the war. "I don't believe they'll ever be used again," he concluded.

Majewski listened attentively. He'd been skeptical about the whole idea, but McNiece's take on it had him reconsidering his opinion. Jake had never steered him wrong, not since the day they'd met at Camp Toccoa.

"I think I'll go back down and talk to Captain Brown again," Majewski said. "You've probably got this figured out right. I'm going too."

McNiece hadn't wanted to influence him. "This is just what I believe," he said. "It is not firsthand knowledge. I can't give you any guarantees."

The private made it clear he didn't need any. He turned and left the barracks, gave his acceptance to Brown, and returned minutes later to start packing his own gear bag.

The barracks was a crowded place, and the men had ears, and not much to do at night besides keep them perked for the latest buzz. Even as McNiece and Majewski prepared for their morning flight, word that they'd volunteered for Pathfinder training had been racing through the grapevine.

As McNiece later recalled, Jack Agnew didn't bother discussing it with him before he marched out to Brown's office.

"Are McNiece and Majewski really going?" he asked.

"Yeah," the captain replied.

Agnew only needed a minute to reach his decision. *Hell*, he thought. *Jake's not going without me.*

A few minutes later, he returned to the barracks, told McNiece he was coming along, and got busy packing. Two more demo men, a "kid" named William Coad and John Dewey, decided to go along too.

They were gathered in McNiece's hut later that night when Lieutenant Williams came through the door. "What's the deal here?" he asked. "I'm losing half my demolition platoon!"

McNiece told him why they'd all shared in his decision. As Agnew would have said about "Little Willie," he was a good officer because he *listened* to his men. Jake figured he deserved to hear it straight.

"It isn't foolproof," McNiece concluded. "But it's almost. I don't think any one of us will ever jump again."

Williams didn't take long to ponder the idea. He went back to Toccoa with the demos, had been through Normandy and Market Garden, and was tired of the war.

"If you guys are going, I'm going too!" he said, hurrying to put his name on the dotted line.

And so early the next morning, six men from the 1st Demolitions Section—including the last original members of the Filthy Thirteen and their lieutenant—left their billet in France on a C-47 transport with a group of other Pathfinder volunteers from the 101st Airborne. While it would not be the only planeload bound for RAF Chalgrove that day, it likely was carrying the happiest, most satisfied man among them.

Jake McNiece had boarded the plane thinking he'd not only matched the United States Army at its own game, but outplayed it, hands down.

What he didn't suspect was that the game was about to be drastically changed.

2.

Early night of December 8, 1944, Captain Frank L. Brown, commanding officer of the newly restructured Pathfinder Company, was in his office at RAF Chalgrove feeling dissatisfied, not to say unhappy, about some things of great importance to him. A short while ago, his fresh crop of eleven officers and eighty-nine men from the 101st Airborne Division had landed at his base for training as Pathfinders, having made the flight from Mourmelon aboard a small fleet of Joel Crouch's IX TCC transports. Their arrival had given him a lot to ponder.

Brown understood that, in one respect, he had every reason to be pleased. He'd been eager to secure replacements for the men who'd been either lost in Holland or had opted out of the group—a soldier's commitment to Pathfinder duty only extended to a particular jump, after which he could ask for reassignment to a different unit. The trainees, then, had been sent at his specific request, with a similar number of volunteers from the 82nd Airborne slated to arrive within four days, for a total of more than two hundred recruits.

From that perspective, the headquarters of the XVIII Airborne Corps was giving him exactly what he needed. But looking at it another way, Brown had no doubt that his request had come as a convenient opening for other officers down the line to rid themselves of their worst, most persistent nuisances and embarrassments.

In hindsight, he might have seen it coming. In mid-October, Major General Maxwell Taylor, the 101's appointed commander, had distributed a stern memorandum titled "PILLAGING AND PLUNDERING (LOOTING)" that he insisted be read by every current and future officer of the division. This had followed complaints from Dutch officers about incidents in and around the village of Heteren, which had been occupied by elements of the 501st PIR before they were relieved by the British.

While Taylor had apologized for the damage to the town, he'd felt there was no evidence to substantiate the accusations and exclude "civilians as well as troops of various organizations" other than the 101st from blame—and had, in fact, told the Dutch their claims were "irresponsible." At the same time, he'd written the memo to inform his officers that "instances of pillaging, plundering and similar offenses" had recently come to his attention, and to remind them that those crimes were punishable by death under military law. But Taylor hadn't stopped there. Making it clear he expected anyone with knowledge of such conduct to take action, he added that commanders would be held accountable for the conduct of their units, and that anyone who proved negligent in the discovery and suppression of looting would be "summarily relieved of command" and have "appropriate disciplinary action" taken against them.

The general's unambiguous warning had prompted the recipients of his memo to clean house of troopers they thought could bring trouble down on their heads—and they'd quickly gone about encouraging or outright pressuring them to volunteer for the Path-finder program.

Brown didn't appreciate having their problems dumped on his shoulders. The Pathfinders had always been a landing spot for guys who flouted authority. Guys who hadn't been good at obeying rules, but who'd mostly been good *combat soldiers* . . . men who were capable of receiving instruction, fought hard, and could be trusted to do the job when it counted. While the current batch had a few reliable holdovers from Normandy and Holland, a glance at their files suggested that too many of them had been selected without regard for their qualifications. Brown had serious reservations about their ability to be competent and dependable Pathfinders.

That was the reason he'd summoned Jake McNiece into his office on this cold, blustery Friday evening. McNiece was the furthest thing imaginable from a choirboy. But his Filthy Thirteen had gained quite the reputation when it came to soldiering, one that went far beyond words in a magazine article. In Normandy, they'd blown two bridges and held one against vastly superior numbers. And they'd performed no less ably and courageously in Holland, with two-thirds of their platoon sacrificing their lives in combat.

Brown needed McNiece, needed him badly. And he would not be shy about letting him know it.

He was ready when his aide showed the sergeant through the door. His uniform rumpled, his hair disheveled (he no longer wore a scalplock), a dark scruff of beard shadowing his cheeks, McNiece looked exactly as Brown had imagined. It encouraged him that they might indeed be kindred spirits under the skin.

"What's your big problem?" McNiece said, taking a seat front of his desk. "I just got here at five o'clock this evening and went to bed. I don't know what your big deal is but I did not do it and wasn't even involved."

Brown looked at him. "McNiece, I don't know you or anything about you," he said. "I know you are a goof-off or you wouldn't be here. But I need an acting first sergeant and you've been recommended."

McNiece's expression hung somewhere between amusement and disbelief. "Boy, somebody's been pulling your leg," he said. "I've been here for nearly three years and haven't made private first class yet. I don't care about garrison soldiering or military discipline or courtesies or that sort of thing. I'd have my arm fall off before I would salute an officer. I would not pick up a cigarette butt if you all were going to put me in chains. I don't go for any of that. I don't care about that whole malarkey. You don't want me as the first sergeant. I'm not first sergeant material. I'm the biggest goof-off in the army."

Brown listened calmly, his eyes on McNiece's face, waiting for the right moment to make his pitch. "I'm here for the same reason you are," he said, sensing he'd reached it. "*I'm* a goof-off just like you. We've got four hundred goof-offs here—a hundred from the One-Oh-First, a hundred from the Eighty-Second, a hundred from the Seventeenth, and a hundred foreigners. They told me you've been through this thing from Normandy on through, and made two jumps, and that you could whip this deal into shape and get it right and ready quick. That's what I want."

The captain fell silent. The number of jumps wasn't the important thing, of course. McNiece was not alone in that distinction, and they both knew it. The crux of it was that Brown wanted someone the Pathfinders would trust with their lives, and whose leadership *he* could trust. You could call McNiece a lot of things that weren't too flattering and they would all be true. But the man was fearless and would do whatever was necessary to reach his objective—and that made him a damn good soldier. Brown's instincts told him he was the right man for the job.

McNiece sat there digesting his words. "It sounds like we might be dealing on the table," he said. "But if I'm going to do this, I want my men treated halfway reasonable for a change. We have never had a square meal since we went in the Army three years ago. I want good food. I want good quarters, and I want these people to have an almost permanent pass as long as they'll respect it. And the first thing they're going to do is take a three-day pass to London."

Brown didn't know about that one. London offered far too many opportunities for them to get into hot water. "That may be beyond my line of reason, McNiece," he said. "How many of these guys do you think we'd get back?"

"You'll get back all of them except the ones that are in jail. And just as quick as the bobbies notify us, we'll go get them. Most of these boys are fine soldiers . . . they're just field soldiers, not garrison. They are a good bunch of men. They've been behind enemy lines for seventy-two days. They need to get into town and let off some steam."

The captain only needed to think about it for another moment.

"Well, I'll tell you what I'll do," he said. "I'll get you a passbook and you can let everybody in here have a three-day pass without destination."

McNiece looked satisfied with that, and why not? He'd mainly gotten what he'd wanted. But Brown wasn't finished. This was all about trust. If they were going to build some between them, it had to extend both ways.

"You've got to stay here, get these sticks organized, and get a training program set up," he went on. "You're going to have to pick yourself out a stick. You'll all stay here the three days while the others are gone and familiarize yourselves with the organization and objectives. When they get back, then you can go."

McNiece was still bargaining. "Okay," he said. "I'll be the first sergeant under that kind of a deal."

That wasn't a request Brown was prepared to grant . . . not that he found it unreasonable. Most military units had a table of organization that broke down the kind of staffing they were to be provided— the number of officers, noncoms, and enlisted men needed to fill their structural requirements. In a typical unit, the responsibilities McNiece was being asked to take on would have fallen to a first sergeant. But there was no TO for the Pathfinders. They were not permanently assigned to IX TCC Pathfinder Group, but had been placed on temporary duty for what had, under its reorganization, become an accelerated two-week rather than a two-month training period.

Based on all that, Brown explained that if McNiece was to receive a boost in rank—and pay—to sergeant it would be up to his commanding officer at HQ/501 to recommend one. He did not believe he had the authority.

"You'll serve the same grade you came in," he said. Meaning he would remain a private essentially performing the duties of a sergeant, but without an official promotion.

McNiece didn't put up an argument. The pay commensurate with a boost in rank hadn't been important to him. "Let me jump in where there's money and I'll get my own pay raises," he said.

Brown knew he was referring to his demo team's ability to blow safes at will but correctly dismissed the comment as bluster. His instincts were right on target. Although he had no way to know it, McNiece never expected to make a combat jump again.

McNiece left the office with the passbook and gave out furloughs to all the recruits except those he'd selected for his stick. These were guys from his regiment, and guys he considered the cream of the crop. He knew he was far from expert on everything, and wanted men who knew what they knew. He also wanted demo-sabos with him, thinking that if a DZ or LZ was mined, they would be able to clear the area fast. That placed Agnew, and the kid, Dewey, at the top of his list. McNiece chose T-5 George Blain, a fellow Toccoa man, because he'd been a Pathfinder in Normandy and Holland and had experience with the Eureka box. The rest of the team were solid, all-around soldiers he'd known awhile, and in some cases fought beside—Sergeant Cleo Merz, Sergeant Leo Schulenburg, and Private George Slater. Since nominal command of every stick went to a commissioned officer, he would request, and get, Lieutenant Schrable Williams for his team leader.

With Pathfinder doctrine calling for redundancy built upon redundancy, McNiece chose a backup team whose performance he felt would approach his own in the heat of battle. Once again putting together a mix of seasoned Pathfinders, demos, and combat veterans, he strongly weighed his selections toward guys from Toccoa. Corporal Richard "Red" Wright, Corporal Carl Fenstermaker, Private Lachlan "Mac" Tillman, and Private Lavon P. Reese all went back a long way and were original Pathfinders, the first three having survived the crash of their transport when it ditched on D-Day Minus One. Private Mathon Ferster, Private Floyd

Thomas, and Private Irv Schumacher, rounding out the stick's enlisted men, were also battle-tested guys who would hold up under fire. Lieutenant Gordon Rothwell, who'd been CO on the downed Normandy flight and led a stick of Pathfinders into Holland, would repeat his role as team leader for a third time. His scorn for officers aside, McNiece figured it counted for something that Rothwell had never lost a man.

The last guy he chose for this secondary team was Max Majewski. One of the best soldiers he'd ever met, Max had changed after his wife got sick and died back home—become kind of unbalanced. His temper was on a short fuse, and you never knew what would set it off. That was why Gene Brown had wanted him out of his hair, and Jake had hardly been able to blame him. It was the same reason he'd decided against putting him on his own stick.

Max was a concern, no two ways about it. He knew he'd have to keep a close eye on him.

As Pathfinder school got under way in the second week of December, Brown and McNiece would have to deal with some early snafus to keep it on schedule. One source of frustration was an arctic storm front that would bring heavy snows to the British countryside, blanketing it with whiteness and grounding the practice flights. This would force the men to drill with their light panels and dummy Eurekas under conditions that didn't quite duplicate the rigors of jumping with the equipment. But there was nothing to do but work around Mother Nature when she refused to cooperate.

Brown did get one problem rectified after he noticed the men had arrived at Chalgrove poorly clothed and supplied. Coming out of Market Garden, they were in uniforms and undergarments that were worn, threadbare, and falling apart at the seams, with only a few of the troopers lucky enough to still have their sleeping bags. McNiece was wearing the same boots he'd had on through Normandy and Holland, and had patched quarter-sized holes in their bottoms with pasteboard.

Though Brown understood that requisitions were backlogged following the Holland campaign, he'd found this unacceptable and gotten his quartermaster to press the Army for urgently needed replacements. By late December their tenacity had paid off. The station was given high priority for shipments of supplies, and all the Pathfinders were clothed and equipped up to standards.

Another issue Brown dealt with as the course progressed was attrition. By late December, he and McNiece had booted fifteen troopers—two officers and six enlisted men from the 101st and six enlisted men from the 82nd—from Pathfinder school for ineptitude or breaches of conduct. This number was higher than the normal rate of dismissal, and Brown would blame it on the quality of some of the recruits selected for the training—in other words, dumped in his lap—by their commanding officers. But with both divisions in combat, and those COs having cleaned house of their worst problems, his requests for substitutes were ignored . . . and intentionally so, he suspected.

Repaying their consideration in kind, Brown shipped the castoffs back to their parent units in a hurry, caustically explaining in each instance that it didn't seem advisable to keep men who "weren't qualified for instruction" at his base when they were needed for combat duty. Later on, in a report to Major General Matthew Ridgeway of the Eighth Airborne Corps, he would request that more consideration be given to the selection process "in order to provide competent and dependable Pathfinders."

In polite terms, he was telling the commander of all airborne forces in Europe that he'd had his fill of inheriting other officers' rejects and wanted that to change.

For his part, McNiece was okay with the guys he had available, and remained convinced the war would be over long before they brought their training to the battlefield. But a deal was a deal, and he stuck to it, working the men hard until he was satisfied they knew what they were doing.

Near the end of the two-week course, a group of Air Force officers arrived to watch the men showcase their use of the navigational beacons. Naturally, one of the lieutenant-colonels asked Majewski, of all those he *could* have asked, to demonstrate the operation of the AN/CRN-4 homing transmitter, a smaller, lighter, trimmed-down version of the Eureka the group had been practicing with in the field. The same device that had brought in the gliders in Market Garden, it would now be used exclusively by the Pathfinders—although they'd only been given dummy models for training purposes.

McNiece drew a breath. The CRN-4 had a single button you needed to press for a signal, and that was it. But while Max had come through the course all right, he was still kind of unpredictable.

"It will send signals so the pilots can pick you up with their sets," he explained, and then crouched over the controls. "This button here, you just press it on and off, on and off, on and off."

The officer looked at him. "You mean intermittently?" he asked.

Majewski screwed up his face. "Let me see," he said. "On and off, on and off. Yeah, Colonel, that would be intermittently, I think."

The officer ignored the gibe—or possibly it went right over his head. Either way, he didn't say anything about it.

McNiece exhaled. The truth was that pushing those two buttons was all he and Max knew about the Eureka. Blain was the expert and that was fine with them. Besides, as far as Jake was concerned, their use of the radar and lights would never go further than demonstrations. He was as confident as ever that the Pathfinders and the rest of the Army would be returning to the States before long.

December was now entering its third week. With Western Europe encased in snow and ice, and Hitler's lines pulled so far back that the Allies had established footholds in Germany's western territories, the war front was quiet. Confident the lull would last until the spring thaw, and that the bad weather areas were unlikely to see German counteroffensives, the American and British high commands had left them thinly patrolled.

Earlier in the month, General Taylor had taken advantage of the hard-earned break in the action and left the 101's billet at Mourmelon for a working visit to the States. His trip began with a half-hour meeting at the Pentagon on December 10, where he and Army Chief of Staff George C. Marshall had an exchange of ideas about the future nature of airborne deployments. A day later, he was extensively debriefed about Market Garden by Secretary of War Henry Stimpson, touching on the Dutch allegations of trooper misbehavior, among many other subjects. Taylor's main order of business, however, was a conference with senior operations officers about a plan he'd developed to overhaul the staffing of airborne divisions.

On December 15, Marshall approved most of his recommendations and sent him off on a tour of training installations along the East Coast.

That same evening across the Atlantic, the 26th *Volksgrenadier*, a division of the XLVII Panzer Corps, had begun gathering on the German side of the Our River, which drew a crooked line through the Ardennes mountain range along the Fatherland's southwestern border with Belgium. Behind them in the rolling forests of Germany's Eifel region, 500 medium tanks, 900 armored assault guns, 19,000 pieces of artillery, and the bulk of a 200,000-man infantry force had gathered amid the blowing snow.

The troop buildup had gone mostly unnoticed by the Allies. Aerial reconnaissance flights were impossible in the stormy weather, and the U.S. Army's 28th Infantry—its command post located outside a hub town named Bastogne—had seen the Germans assemble on the river's opposite banks before. With its high plateaus, rugged peaks, steep valley walls, and waist-deep snowpack, the terrain had seemed impassable in the winter to SCAEF Eisenhower. Only a single German division was believed to be in the area, and he had felt that the 28th, though depleted from long weeks of bloody battle in the Hürtgen Forest, and filling slowly with green replacements, could adequately patrol the American sector of the border, a twenty-five-mile stretch that was more than three times the area a unit its size should have covered.

It would prove to be a costly misjudgment.

During the final weeks of 1944, Hitler had ensconced himself in the Wolf's Lair, his Prussian headquarters, and devised a plot to strike at the heart of his Western enemies while they slept the sleep of the overconfident, idle in their winter blankets, believing victory in their grasp. His scheme was to drive a massive armored force across the river into Belgium, where he would split the Allied front between American and British lines and retake the strategic port city of Antwerp. And that was only his partial goal.

Divided from one another by the German spearhead, America's First and Ninth Armies, Canada's First Army, and the British Second Army would be encircled and annihilated during the attack, a move intended to rock the Allies' confidence and shatter their unity. Hitler saw the Americans as weak-willed, and felt the stunning defeat would break their resolve and force them to the negotiating table, where he could arrive at a compromise peace agreement and be freed to concentrate on his war in the East with Stalin.

It was an audacious gamble that hearkened back to the Third Reich's early years of blitzkrieg and conquest, when its *Wehrmacht* had rolled through Eastern Europe, taking one country after another with swift lightning strikes. Sparing none of his resources, the Führer had drawn vital manpower and tanks away from the Eastern Front with Russia toward the armored advance.

Standing at the hub of seven roads essential to the movement of his Panzer groups, Bastogne was centered in Hitler's crosshairs. Commanded by General Heinrich Freiherr von Lüttwitz, the XLVII Panzers meant to capture it in the first twenty-four hours of their push.

By nightfall on December 15, Lüttwitz's engineers had built floating bridges that spanned the Our, and his infantrymen were marching across into Allied territory behind a hard rain of artillery shells. Among them were infiltrators in American army uniforms, who cut telephone lines to knock out communications and throw the enemy into disarray. As shocked 28th Division patrols made isolated sightings of German troops over the next twenty-four hours, wild skirmishes began to break out in the forests west of Bastogne. On December 17, a U.S. Army field observation battalion was ordered toward the border to establish a defensive position, but was pounced on by a German tank column from *Kamfgruppe Peiper* near the town of Malmédy. Vastly outnumbered and outgunned, the 112 American soldiers who survived the initial attack surrendered to the larger force—after which they were led to a field and massacred in cold blood.

Still, despite their confusion and inexperience, the American troops managed to slow the Germans' progress, with the area's snow-choked roads further impeding it. Lüttwitz's goal had been to take Bastogne on the first day of the operation. But two days later, his tanks remained some miles short of the city's outskirts.

The delay had given Eisenhower and his top officers a chance to regain their bearings and mobilize reinforcements. On the morning of the 17th, he decided that the 82nd and 101st Airborne Divisions, on reserve status after Market Garden, would be sent to the border territory to repel the German push. He would leave it to two members of his general staff—his chief of staff Lieutenant General Walter "Beetle" Smith and the Royal British Army's Major General Sir John Whiteley—to decide precisely where to position them.

Looking at a map of the area, Whiteley poked a finger at Bastogne.

"I think I should put them there," he said. "This place has the best road net in the area."

Smith nodded. He agreed that the village's radial highway network would be advantageous, allowing them to rapidly go where they were needed.

That night both divisions were alerted that they were to move out of their billeting areas with all due haste. Quartered closest to the Netherlands in Suippes and Sissone, France, the 82nd left at dawn on the 18th in a convoy of trailer trucks, the inclement weather ruling out an airborne drop. En route, their destination was changed to the town of Werbomont, where *Kamfgruppe Peiper* had penetrated the American lines.

The 101st departed from Camp Mourmelon later that evening. With Major General Taylor away in the United States, and his assistant division commander Brigadier General Gerald Higgins in England giving a lecture, the operational leadership of the division fell to artillery commander Brigadier General Anthony B. McAuliffe. When SHAEF ordered him to Belgium, McAuliffe gathered his officer staff and told them, simply, "All I know of the situation is that there has been a breakthrough and we have got to get up there."

The men scrambled to pack their bags and ammunition. Although many were on furlough in Paris, McAuliffe didn't wait for them to return. The situation was too urgent.

The 101st left France on the afternoon of the 18th and rode straight through the night, its trucks rumbling through curtains of fog, drizzle, and sleet, their headlights cutting through the gloom despite blackout orders. McAuliffe had instructed his division to head to Werbomont, but after the 82nd was diverted to that village, their destinations were switched. The Screaming Eagles would now roll through the high country into Bastogne and establish it as their base camp.

At 6 A.M. on the morning of December 19, the division's 501st PIR, riding at the head of the convoy, entered the village and went on to the division's assembly point at an outer crossroads. Later on that morning, they were joined there by the rest of the 101st.

With McAuliffe present and in charge, the division would now dig in, establish its perimeter defenses, and try and find out what the Germans planned to do next.

3.

The IX TCC had inherited Chalgrove Airfield from several squadrons of the United States Army Air Force's 10th Reconnaissance Group, a few elements of which still occupied sections of the base. At one-thirty in the afternoon on Friday, December 22, Jake McNiece was walking along the Pathfinder company street when Lieutenant Williams came his way.

"Jake, you need to report to the airfield in half an hour," he said without preamble. "Have your stick ready to jump."

McNiece stood there in the middle of the path, hands deep in his pockets, vapor puffing from his nose, his cheeks numb from the bitter cold.

He spread his hands to indicate the tall heaps of plowed and windblown snow on either side of them.

"Willy, the snow's ass deep to a tall Indian," he said. "What are you thinking to jump in these conditions when every one of the men has forty, fifty jumps? They don't need this. You'll get backs broken, legs broken." He paused, figuring Williams had gotten his orders from Captain Brown. "Tell the captain we're not doing it on account of the weather—"

Williams interrupted him. "Yeah, you are. But not here. It's a combat mission."

McNiece gave him a questioning look. "What are you talking about?"

"I told you. We're going on a combat mission. Two o'clock this afternoon."

Disbelief overspread McNiece's features. A moment ago he'd been thinking about a Christmas furlough in London. What kind of horseshit was this? Did Williams not remember that they'd come from Mourmelon so that they would never have to make another combat jump as long as they lived?

"This mission." he said. "When are we going to be briefed about it?"

"They'll brief you in the plane."

Jake stared at him. He wanted no part of any mission. "Do you know that not a man in the outfit has any combat equipment?" he asked. And he wasn't exaggerating about the equipment. The guys had come to Chalgrove for training purposes and hadn't been issued helmets or field uniforms. Furthermore, with limited facilities for the secure storage of weapons and ammunition, Brown had arranged for the Pathfinder trainees to leave their firearms with their units in France. "We don't even have a CRN-4 that isn't a dummy . . ."

"They're working on it right now," Williams said, quashing his argument. "They'll be at the plane."

They. McNiece suddenly knew this was coming from higher up the ladder than Brown. In fact, he wondered where the captain was. Under the circumstances, he would have expected him to be around.

"You're really serious about this," he said, finally surrendering to the idea.

Williams nodded in the affirmative. "And you haven't heard the worst of it," he said. "Be at the orderly room with your stick in thirty minutes. We'll have jeeps to run you all out to the plane."

It turned out to be a single truck, but Williams was otherwise right on. As the group pulled to a halt at the tarmac where a C-47 was on the runway with its engines warming up, McNiece saw the navigation equipment and other gear waiting to be loaded aboard. Also there to meet the bewildered Pathfinders were a couple of USAAF colonels with the collars of their field overcoats pulled up and grave, no-nonsense looks on their faces.

They.

The officers thrust their arms out and shook hands with McNiece as the troopers and aircrew lifted the gear onto the idling transport.

"Good luck," one of them said.

"What do you mean 'good luck'?" McNiece asked point-blank. He'd about run out of patience. "Where are we going and what's the deal? When do we get briefed?"

The colonel reached into his coat pocket and brought out a folded map. Jake thought it looked like an Automobile Club of America road map. There was nothing detailed about it at all.

"Right now," he said, unfolding it. "You see that circle?"

"Yeah." McNiece said. Using a typical mile-per-inch measure, he estimated the area inside the circle was two miles in diameter, and enclosed a part of Luxembourg, Belgium, situated right at the

German border. He could see what might have been roads or highways spreading out from its center like bicycle spokes.

"That's a town called Bastogne," the colonel explained. "Your division is cut off in there and completely encircled . . . or they were the last time we heard from them. That was two days ago. Whether or not they're still there, I don't know. But all indications are they still are."

McNiece stood quietly under a leaden sky, northeasterly winter gusts beating against his face as they swept across the runway area. There had been no jump for the division. If there had been, he would have known about it. For one thing, the Pathfinders would have been sent in advance to mark their DZs. But that hadn't happened. A mass drop in those mountains out there, with all that snow around, was impossible.

That meant they'd been activated out of reserve status and trucked in from Mourmelon, and something like that only would have happened if the outfits that were already in Bastogne were in a desperate predicament.

"They're out of ammunition, medicine, and food, and have nothing but a handful of men," the colonel went on. "We have to maintain control of Bastogne."

McNiece listened carefully, the reality of the situation sinking in. Being surrounded was nothing new for guys from the 101st. They'd been surrounded all through Normandy. But his gut feeling was that they wouldn't have had much of a chance to prepare themselves for action or load up on provisions and ammo before they moved out. They had been short on stores in the first place—Jake knew because he'd left Mourmelon with torn long johns and holes in his boots just two weeks before. For the boys who'd been

227

ringed in, this wasn't about their holding the village. It was about the Germans having them in a chokehold, and them having no way to fight their way out of it without bullets for their guns and morphine and sulfa for their wounds.

For those men—his friends and brothers—it was about survival. But if the colonel wanted his Pathfinders marking the field for an aerial resupply, it would have to be one hell of a good-sized drop to be of any use to them.

Though he didn't know it, there was a large store of supplies on hand. Weeks earlier, Joel Crouch had made a pair of special recommendations. One was that two sticks of Pathfinders from each airborne division be retained at Chalgrove when their training period concluded in the event a situation occurred demanding their use on the Western Front. The other was that a hundred aircraft loads of vital troop provisions be sent to the air base, pre-bundled for rapid parachute delivery to any unit of the Airborne Corps on request.

Captain Brown had endorsed both ideas. The first had needed approval from the separate divisional commanders—if he was going to keep their men at his base as standbys, they had to sign off on it. But he'd needed no one's permission to implement Crouch's bid for supplies and had procured them from the 490th Quartermaster Company for storage at the airfield.

What Crouch had done with these proposals was create the basis for an unprecedented utilization of the Pathfinders—and in doing so he had taken a large step toward reconceptualizing airborne operations as a whole. Sending them to prepare the drop zones for massive deliveries of airborne troops and gliders had been an innovation, and a successful one, but their previous jumps over

Normandy and Holland had been executed in advance of a main wave of thousands of troopers. The Pathfinders had been a forward component of a larger force. The thought that one or two sticks of paratroopers might be dropped behind enemy lines with a precise, limited tactical objective, delivered for a commando-style mission without follow-on airborne troops, was something altogether new in warfare.

Crouch had understood this. He'd ambitiously pushed the development of airborne operations his entire military career and wanted to keep exploring their tactical possibilities.

Jake McNiece's concerns were different, and perhaps more centered on the moment. Standing on the airfield, the transport waiting behind him, he knew his men were being asked to do something that hadn't been asked of anyone before, and without the benefit of a proper briefing, or a decent recon map of the DZ, or anything close to up-to-the-minute intelligence. He didn't care for it all, but also knew it had to done—though he would not have admitted it to the colonel, who'd tucked away the map and put his hand back out.

"Well," he said again, "good luck."

McNiece had a feeling of déjà vu. "I don't need luck, I need a miracle," he said. "You are trying to hit a two-mile-diameter circle, flying four hundred miles to it in a C-47 that has no navigational aids or instruments."

The colonel looked at him expressionlessly. "Pretty tough deal, boy," he said. "But that's the way it is."

And with that he ended their conversation. It was now a little before three o'clock in the afternoon, and the aircrew was ready to go wheels up.

The Pathfinders climbed aboard, and a few minutes later were in the sky. Lieutenant Williams outlined the mission for the men soon after takeoff. "They went into Bastogne with maybe two or three clips of ammo for every man and hardly anything to wear or eat," he said about their fellow Screaming Eagles. "It could be they've been overrun by Krauts. But we're going to parachute into the encirclement, and set up our equipment if we land in friendly territory, and prepare to bring in vital supplies."

Williams's assessment was off only insofar as the shortage of ammunition, and only by a little. The actual reports from Colonal Kohls, the division supply officer, were that each trooper was down to about ten clips. In practical terms that wasn't much better.

Listening, Jack Agnew became grimly concerned about his buddies in the 506th. When he glanced over at the others, their faces told him they felt the same way.

They flew for about two or three hours, the heavy fog, sleet, and snow wiping out all visibility. Every so often the clouds would break so McNiece was able to make out a patch of ground below, but then the cover would close up on itself and everything would get swept back into the grayness.

He and Agnew would later recall the pilot having contact with someone on the ground before flashing the red light. The tension in the troop compartment had thickened until it felt like jelly in the air around them. Then, as they got ready to stand up, the light blinked off, and the crew chief appeared from the cabin to inform them the plane was returning to base.

Puzzled, McNiece went forward to ask the pilot what was going on. He replied that he'd thought he had nearly reached Bastogne, but then realized he had overshot it by thirty-five miles. He'd still been looking for the town when Captain Brown radioed from Chalgrove and ordered him to cancel the mission.

McNiece was almost surprised by the sinking feeling inside him. But glancing around at the men, studying their faces, he realized every one of them shared his disappointment over the scrub. It was a funny thing too. They'd volunteered to become Pathfinders so they could eat good Air Force food, drink strong English whiskey, and chase pretty Oxford girls. None had ever expected to make another jump. But they were all thinking about the boys down there in Bastogne. And though they hadn't needed to share those thoughts aloud, there wasn't a man in that troop compartment who'd wanted to turn back.

At Chalgrove, meanwhile, Brown was irate. On a rare trip off base when the colonels arrived from Ninth Air Force Headquarters, he hadn't been consulted about the mission, let alone authorized the Pathfinder stick's departure. Nor did he think it was coincidental that the officers had showed up while he was gone. He would subsequently learn that the 101st had radioed an urgent request for supplies to the Eighth Army, which had in turn put its thumb on HQ to fly them in. But given the weather and early sunsets that time of year, he'd felt an afternoon start for the mission was out of the question. The operation would need hours of daylight to have a chance of success.

It was nightfall when the C-47 returned to the station. Waiting on the tarmac, Brown watched McNiece climb down the ladder and then approach him in the swirling mist.

"Let's hit the mess, then all go into the operations room," he said, slouching under his equipment load. "See what the best plan of attack is."

The captain agreed. After wolfing down a hot dinner, the men gathered together amid the room's map tables and wall charts. Joining them there were members of the base's G-2 Intelligence section.

"I think we ought to take two planeloads of men next time," McNiece told the group. With weather conditions being so poor, he saw a strong chance of losing a plane. And that was before taking enemy interference into consideration. "I'll be in the first one."

Brown would have recommended that himself. Two sticks not only made practical sense, it was in full keeping with Pathfinder operational doctrine.

"We've got a crackerjack pilot," he offered. "A guy who can hit that place easily."

McNiece gave him a look. "I hope so," he said. "Since you missed it by thirty-five miles today, everyone would be a little happier if you *could* get somebody who could put me in or near Bastogne."

The captain didn't comment. He did, in fact, have the fleet's best transport pilot on board for the drop. And maybe the best flying ace in the USAAF, period.

"You'll need a predetermined signal," he said. "Something to show the second load of men you're in friendly territory."

McNiece thought about that. "I'll take black and orange smoke grenades," he said. Orange was the Netherlands' national color, and the same color smoke the Pathfinders had used in Market. The Germans wouldn't use it, so there would be no mistaking who was sending it up. "If it looks feasible that we could get in and start a resupply mission, I will throw out orange smoke grenades. When the pilots see it, they're to drop Rothwell's stick right on top of me."

He paused. "Black smoke means danger or disaster. If it's a hopeless case and they see black, forget about us. Try to relocate and drop the men somewhere else."

Brown nodded, and so did Lieutenant Williams. Agnew had always thought the thing that made Little Willy a good officer was that he listened to his men. And he'd listened that night. In fact, everyone in the room had listened to Jake that night. There was a kind of resolve in it that was contagious.

Their takeoff was set for 6:45 in the morning, and the men turned in to their barracks. The next day was going to be a long one for the Pathfinders. Although not many of them figured to get much sleep, they would at least have mattresses under their backs and blankets to cover themselves with, and they knew that it might be a while until they enjoyed those comforts again.

Or might be the last time ever.

CHAPTER SEVEN

1.

McNiece had hit his bunk after the briefing in the operations room knowing he'd lied outright to everybody there—his men, the officers, everyone. And boarding the plane at a little before six o'clock the next morning, he'd continued the lie without a shred of guilt.

For all his talk about black and orange smoke grenades, he hadn't carried any black ones with him. Bringing them along had sounded good at the time, though he'd probably just come up with it to satisfy Captain Brown and the G-2 boys. The brass always needed contingencies to keep them happy, and he'd served them one for dessert.

But he couldn't go into this mission thinking it had a chance to fail, or that there was really a fallback open to him. He couldn't approach it like that and leave room for doubt in his heart. When the first plane carrying him to Bastogne had aborted its run the day before, something had told him he'd have to make the next go at it work no matter what it took. He'd felt it right away, and Jack Agnew had too. It hadn't been long after they'd turned back toward England that Jack said they'd been wrong to quit. That they should have kept looking for the town.

So McNiece hadn't carried those black smoke grenades. Since he wouldn't be using them, he'd figured why bother? Besides, his allocated load of grenades was supposed to be ten and ten, and common sense told him the smoke from twenty orange grenades would be easier to spot from the air. When he set them off, he wanted to look like "an orange juice tank truck exploding" among the thousands upon thousands of German soldiers around him.

Whatever it took. That morning, McNiece had left the barracks early for a preflight briefing that had given him plenty to think about on that score. There had been a few more trickles of intelligence coming out of Bastogne overnight, and most of it was bad. But the briefing gave him a fuller understanding of what was going on there, and how the 101st had gotten into such an awful jam.

One thing he'd learned was that the 28th Infantry had been holding the town before they were sent in. But there weren't many seasoned men left in that division after the Hürtgen Forest bloodbath in November, and most of those soldiers were replacements from the States, kids who hadn't fought a day in the war. The German Panzer divisions that punched through the lines had come at them like a giant battering ram, and when Eisenhower heard about it, he'd called in the airborne to form a perimeter around the town.

As Jake had already guessed, the weather had ruled out a jump. On December 18, the eleven thousand troopers at Mourmelon had been packed like cattle into almost four hundred trailer trucks and moved out to become part of that defensive ring. But they'd brought next to nothing in the way of supplies, and hadn't been briefed on the situation they were heading into. The 101st would reach Bastogne only to learn that they and rest of the American troops were outnumbered three to one.

By the 19th they'd been surrounded by German tank and infantry outfits. McNiece's own 506th had taken heavy casualties holding off a Panzer group east of town, losing about a third of its six hundred troopers in forty-eight hours. They'd done worse damage to the enemy, taking out about thirty of their tanks and a thousand men, but on December 20 they'd had to pull back. It seemed as if there was no end to the German forces. They were getting closer and closer every day, shrinking the circle around the troops.

It was an understatement to say the weather wasn't making things easier for them. On the 21st it had started snowing, and the snow had kept piling up as the temperature dropped, and now the men were freezing in over a foot of it. They had no winter linings for their boots. They had no long johns. They didn't even have blankets to wrap themselves in.

None of it made sense to McNiece. He couldn't see how the Allied High Command had gotten caught so badly off guard. But he wasn't Eisenhower or Montgomery, and it wasn't his job to figure it out. He already had enough on his plate.

Now several hours into the flight, he sat in the C-47's troop compartment, feeling restless although he'd barely shut his eyes all night and then gotten summoned into the briefing before sunrise. Soon after takeoff, he'd moseyed forward to introduce himself to Brown's crackerjack pilot. His name was Lieutenant Joel Crouch, and he'd supposedly written the book on Pathfinding, not that it meant a lot to Jake under the circumstances. He'd never paid much attention to the books.

"You don't have much confidence in this, do you?" Crouch asked when he entered the cabin.

McNiece considered his question. He'd mostly developed the mission plan, and wouldn't have expected his men to follow a plan he didn't believe in. *Confidence?* Maybe it ought to have been him asking that of the pilot.

"Change that to 'little or no,' confidence," he lied. "I got carried on a merry chase yesterday, and I'm expecting the same thing today. I don't think you can hit Bastogne."

Lieutenant Crouch looked at him over his shoulder, his hands on the controls. This was the same man of whom journalist Lorelle Hearst, on meeting him shortly before the D-Day Pathfinder drop, had written: *Although I had no idea {his mission} was going to be that important, I instinctively knew it would be something very brave . . . You are going to hear a great deal more about him, because he is terrific . . . absolutely tops at his job.*

McNiece had not read Hearst's story about Crouch in the stateside newspaper. But he was a sharp judge of character, and the pilot's quiet charisma and poised self-assurance likely impressed him much as it had the reporter. He decided to play along and see what Crouch could do.

In the copilot's seat, meanwhile, Vito Pedone had gotten a look on his face that said he was no stranger to the game.

"At eight-fifteen on the dot I'll pull us down out of this fog," Crouch said. "We'll be over Lille, France. You can check on the flight map."

"Good." McNiece had deliberately sounded skeptical.

They'd flown on for a while. Right at a quarter past eight Crouch banked gently down to a low altitude and Lille was below them.

McNiece thought that was a nice stunt.

"The next place we'll hit is Luxembourg," the pilot said, and gave another time of arrival.

McNiece looked at him. "Sure," he said.

At the exact time he'd mentioned, Crouch shaved altitude again. They were over Luxembourg.

Their gazes had briefly met, and McNiece had tried not to look too impressed.

"Well," McNiece said. "This gives me a little more hope."

He'd stood there in the cabin as Crouch brought the plane back up.

"In about fifteen minutes, I'm going to give you a green light," the pilot said. "Now get out of here. If you do your job, I'll do mine."

McNiece had just given him a nod, turned, and gone back to rejoin his men. That had been a short while ago. It was almost nine o'clock in the morning now, and the two Pathfinder planes were nearing their destination. They'd had smooth flying the entire trip, but McNiece expected the situation to get hot when they got closer to the DZ. With the resupply planes in the air waiting for his signal, there would be no room for error, and no time for it, either.

He guessed he'd see how things turned out, though it was fair to say that Crouch was well off his list of concerns. Whatever happened, he felt confident the ol' boy could handle it.

2.

Completing his long turn over Belgium, Lieutenant Crouch descended from the clouds toward the wide plateau where Bastogne perched amid the snow-mantled Ardennes forests. He would been more comfortable if their promised Ninth Air Force fighter escort had materialized over Reims, where they'd been supposed to rendezvous. The planes hadn't been there as specified, however, and he'd been unable to wake up anyone at the base—or so it seemed, since no one answered his radio calls. It had left him with no choice but to continue without them.

A few minutes after nine o'clock he brought the transport down through the cloud cover to treetop level.

What he and Pedone saw below was in a very real sense the opposite of what they remembered from D-Day Minus One, when they had looked down on the vast Allied armada stretching from one side of the Channel to the other. Now all the two men could make out were German troops, armor, and artillery surrounding Bastogne like a vast sea rising up around a tiny island, threatening to inundate its shores.

Crouch knew the Pathfinders in the troop compartment would be jumping into the middle of that fearsome assembly, and without up-to-date intelligence to tell them whether they'd land in enemy or American-held territory. He respected that sort of courage above all else, and nothing could have stopped him from flying them in himself. Every one of his pilots was capable in his opinion. But the moment Brown had told him about the mission, he'd known he had to do it.

He craned his head to look out his windscreen, peering past the inner edge of the German buildup at the town proper. One of the main landmarks G-2 had told him to seek out was a large cemetery. The area Colonel Kohls had suggested for the DZ was just outside it, between two lines of American resistance—assuming they'd continued to hold out against the pressing German force. No one had heard from Kohls for some time.

Crouch nodded to Pedone. He could see the cemetery straight ahead, so at least he knew they were on course. The copilot nodded back, toggling on the green light above the jump door.

In the troop compartment, Schrable Williams had just ordered the men to stand up and hook up when the ground fire started pouring up around them. They could see tracers whizzing past the windows, burning so hot they were visible in broad daylight. Then the guns seemed to zero in on the transport, their 88mm rounds striking its thin metal skin with rapid *takking* sounds.

McNiece was standing in front of Sergeant Cleo Merz as he prepared to jump. He thought Merz was one of the nicest fellows he'd met in the service, and got a kick of how the little guy always seemed to have a smile tugging at his lips, like he could see the humor in just about anything. As the flak intensified, they heard a deafening bang in the cabin and flinched. Jake looked around to see that the plane was still in one piece around him, then looked over at the diminutive sergeant and realized his smile had stretched out into a full-blown, rubbery grin. Before McNiece had a chance to wonder what had brought it on, Mertz stuck his finger into a hole in the side of the plane between them. A round had punched right through it and barely missed killing one or the other of them.

McNiece gazed silently down at the ground through a window after that. The mass of German troops and tanks looked like a huge black carpet against the whiteness of the snow, and he could see dead ahead the artillery emplacement that was firing at the transport.

At the controls, Crouch could see it even more clearly. The guns were right in his flight path. He was not going to be able to elude them, and he had no fighter support that could take them out. As far as he could tell that left him with only one option.

Bracing himself in his seat, he nosed into a power dive that hearkened back to his old barnstorming days, looking right down the barrels of those guns.

Caught by surprise, most of the troopers behind him sank to the floor, unable to keep their balance under the tremendous gravitational force produced by the dive. Down on his knees, Agnew saw the Germans leap from the platform of the artillery emplacement and then go scattering off in all directions. Whether they assumed they'd shot the transport out of the air or believed the pilot to be a suicidal lunatic, they'd been convinced he was about to come crashing directly into them.

It was precisely what Crouch had wanted them to think. Streaking past the abandoned artillery guns, he pulled the aircraft sharply up to jump altitude and turned to Pedone again. "As soon as I level off, give them the green light!"

A minute later it flashed on. Barely back on their feet, the troopers went out the door.

3.

As he fluttered to earth, McNiece saw a sprawling cemetery below him, its frozen knolls and lawns studded with elaborate head-stones, footstones, and mausoleums. Its size reassured him they were over Bastogne. No other village in the area would have a burial ground that large, and he was thinking that all those monuments would provide good cover if he landed on top of the Germans.

And then he was down, his boots breaking through the snow crust. He rolled into all that whiteness, wrestled free of the harness and chute, got back on his feet, and shoved his hands into his waist pouches for the smoke grenades. An instant later, he was hurling them everywhere, never mind if there might be enemy guns trained on him, *whump-whump-whump*, churning up a huge orange cloud as he kept lobbing the grenades, one after another after another, Germans be damned, *whump-whump-whump*, everywhere, so it must have looked to the pilots up there overhead like hell was popping its lid around him.

Still hanging from his risers in midair, George Blain, the radar man, saw the thick orange plumes rising up from below and decided not to wait till he was on the ground to give the transports his okay. Hitting the switch on the portable AN/CRN-4 set strapped to his body, he sent the signal and looked up at the orbiting planes with a kind of manic, adrenaline-infused giddiness. *What a party!* he thought.

In his cockpit, Joel Crouch radioed Headquarters to open the aerial supply line. Because he was a precise, thorough man, he'd waited for his Rebecca to interrogate the radar unit, keeping one eye on its cathode ray screen, only sending out the message after he saw the blips. But in a sense that was a technical and procedural formality. It would have been enough for him to see McNiece whip up a billowing orange funnel, flinging his grenades like a man having wild conniptions, his bright, rising smoke signal a clear declaration that he was right where he needed to be.

As he pulled away now, Crouch noticed three or four burning German light tanks not far from where he'd made his pass, a large, undamaged Panzer within four hundred yards of them, and an enemy armored column resting alongside a nearby road. Still on the radio, he relayed the information in the hopes that HQ could get some fighters out—but had no regrets about dropping the troopers. If the bombers came, the armor would be duck soup, and the truth was that he and McNiece weren't that different. Failure hadn't been an option for either man when they left Chalgrove that morning to go sneaking over the German heads. They had come here to get the job done.

Flying behind Crouch, Lieutenant Lionel Wood got the signal and gave the thumbs-up to his copilot, who immediately flashed the green light for their troopers. Both felt as if their nerves had been replaced with high-voltage wires. They had flown Normandy and Market together, and those missions had been hairy, but the one they were on today was somehow different. This time there were thousands of American troops freezing to death down there in the snow, waiting for them, desperate for food, water, medicine, and warm clothing, their lives depending on a handful of men coming down right on a dime.

Behind the cabin bulkhead, Red Wright was having comparable thoughts, praying to God that the planes bringing in his group had the best navigators to ever chart a course through the air. Looking down at the ring of Germans as they'd flown in, it had occurred to him that he would be trying to drop into a doughnut hole maybe a mile and a half across. It had seemed one hell of a long shot.

But then the green light flashed above the door, and just like that, he put all those thoughts aside. The fear that been wriggling in his stomach was gone. Red had promised himself several times that he would make a difference in the battle against Hitler's evil. He had made that promise when he enlisted, and done it again when he ditched into the Channel, and had repeated his promise after he heard that Salty Harris, one of the best friends he'd had in his entire life, was killed by a sniper in Normandy. There was a reason they'd gotten into the war. A reason they were fighting and dying.

Now he heard Lieutenant Rothwell shout, "Go," and turned to Dutch Fenstermaker in line beside him, looked into his eyes, and could see that Dutch knew the same thing he knew: This was it, their turn, their chance.

Red jumped without hesitation as his stick poured out of the transport into a rising cloud of orange smoke.

On the ground, meanwhile, Jack Agnew stood up to get out of his harness with blood sheeting from his nose, mouth, and chin. Right after his chute opened, he'd seen an enemy tank below him—it was the same Panzer Crouch had spotted—and tried to free up his tommy gun, ready for a fight. Though the tank hadn't come close, he'd hit the ground hard and the sub had smashed into his face. A "mess," he went staggering toward the others as they hastily assembled outside the cemetery. With German machine-gun fire and mortar shells raining upon them from about a hundred fifty yards away, they hurried through its gate to take cover, scrambling behind some enormous monuments.

Almost at once, McNiece realized that they were getting screened by fire from deeper inside the graveyard. Then he saw a squad of American troopers come racing over to them. Members of the division's 327th Glider Infantry, they'd held a defensive line there for days and had been on alert for the transports since sunrise. Notified that a second Pathfinder mission had been arranged, Colonel Kohls, the supply officer, had ordered the soldiers to contact him at first sight of the planes.

Kneeling for cover behind a monument, Rothwell suddenly had a field telephone thrust into his hand. It was the colonel.

"How long before the resupply flights arrive?" Kohls asked.

Rothwell told him the first group of planes—forty C-47s from the IX TCC—was circling over France waiting for a signal and would appear within ninety minutes. These would be followed by a second wave of aircraft from the 441st Troop Carrier Group. And there would be more after that. All told there were more than two hundred planes waiting to deliver their loads.

"We need to know where you want us to set up the drop zones," he said over the noise of the volleys.

Kohls had him and Williams brought over to the division's command post on the opposite side of the graveyard so they could figure it out. As the officers sped off through the snow in a waiting jeep, a medic went to work on Agnew. With guns rattling on both sides of the line, McNiece also stayed behind in the cemetery to await instructions.

They came quickly. Phoning from the CP, Williams told him the beacons were to be laid in approximately the same area where the sticks had made landfall. At Chalgrove the Pathfinders had practiced arranging the light panels in circles, and they would build four of them inside the 327's defensive perimeter, one for each ARN/CR-4 unit. It was vital that one beacon be set up to guide in the initial wave of planes, with the others prepared for successive flights. Finally, because it was believed the Germans could home in on their signals, the portable radar sets were only to be turned on when the men heard the incoming resupply aircraft—and no sooner. The instant the primary set was activated, a fleet of jeeps and quarter-ton trucks would zero in on the signal, speed out to the DZ from the command post, and start picking up the urgently needed ammunition, clothing, rations, and medical supplies for distribution to the troops.

With the 327th infantrymen providing cover, McNiece led the men out of the graveyard to look for a place to set up the radar. He spotted a large pile of bricks at the top of a hill and ran over to scout it out more closely. The pile stood across the road from a dilapidated old farmhouse and was about a dozen feet tall and more than twice as long, its bricks carefully stacked for construction. Though it was only about a hundred yards from the German line—the men could see the enemy emplacements with their naked eyes—Jake figured that placing the CR-4 on the brick pile would ensure that it was high enough that nothing would obstruct its signal.

"Climb up on there and get the radar ready," he told Agnew, who was carrying one of his stick's two boxes. He motioned to the snow-crusted ground alongside the pile. "The rest of you lay out the panels."

Agnew searched for a handhold, handed the box to one of the men, stretched his arms above his head, and, groping at the bricks, hoisted himself to the top. A moment later he reached down for the radar.

That was right about when McNiece saw a boy of about fourteen race out the front door of the old farmhouse, cross the road, and come hustling up to the group of Pathfinders and troopers from the 327th.

"What's your name?" he asked the kid.

"Loui," he said, and then gestured that he wanted to help carry the panels.

McNiece watched as the men put him to work, then turned to look around the hill. He needed to decide where to set up the remaining units.

Leaving Wright, Fenstermaker, and most of the other men to lay out the DZ, he hurried off with Blain and the rest to scout out the area. His boots slipping and sliding over the ice and snow, the air so frigid it felt like he was inhaling razor blades, he found three decent locations on two different nearby hills. They set the first box up on a hill outside the farmhouse across the road, then ran up another hill with a big metal storage shed on its crest. The next radar unit was set up on one side of the rise, and the last one on the hilltop directly in front of the shed. The high ground was ideal for the signal, and McNiece figured the building would provide emergency cover for the operator.

The troopers had barely finished setting up that fourth unit when the German guns unleashed a fusillade from their positions behind the line, the ammunition drilling into the snow and clanging against the side of the shed. Taking hurried shelter inside, the men heard the whine of incoming artillery shells and then felt explosions shake the ground as they slammed into the hillside. With each volley the blasts got closer.

McNiece was not about to stay there until the Germans zeroed in. He got his men out of the shed fast, shouting at the top of his lungs as he hustled them along, grabbing the radar unit off the ground. They barely escaped before the artillery hit the structure hard, hammering it into a mound of crumpled scrap metal.

It was now a few minutes past eleven in the morning, and McNiece knew the supply transports would be well under way, the IX TCC's planes flying east over the Channel to clip the northern tip of France en route to Belgium, the rest of the armada launching from an airfield outside Paris and swinging in from the west.

Leaving a few men at each of the radar sites, he led the rest of his group back to the brick pile. Unable to do anything but wait there on top of it, Agnew, his teeth chattering from the bitter cold, had been watching American burial details pull the dead from both sides out of the snow and ice, toiling to get the stiff, frozen bodies onto their litters, then carrying them shoulder-high where the drifts were piled deep. He would never forget those things, never forget enduring the dreadful cold out there on those bricks, exposed to the wind and snow, shivering in a field jacket borrowed from the IX TCC air corps.

The men at the pile first heard the C-47s right about when McNiece got back. The unmistakable noise of their engines pulsed in the air, low and then louder. Glancing down at Jake, Agnew knew to wait a little longer to send out the homing signal. Kohls had wanted half an hour's notice to give the trucks time to roll in, and that meant estimating the planes' arrival time. But they would hold off with the radar as long as possible so the Germans couldn't get a fix on them.

They waited, taking sporadic gunfire, the Pathfinders and 327th troopers returning it with their own weapons. Finally, at about eleven-twenty, McNiece gave the nod, and Agnew's hand went to the switch.

The sound of the cargo aircraft a droning wave overhead, all eyes turned toward the west.

4.

The forty C-47s of the IX TCC had taken off from Chalgrove in three-ship Vs, traveling through clouds and fog so thick the air-crews had to rely on their instruments to maintain course and altitude.

Today even the birds are walking, thought Lieutenant Art Fei-gion, who was piloting a transport in the third serial. He'd flown Normandy with the Pathfinders, and a mission conducted in instrument weather was therefore nothing new to him, but the near-whiteout conditions were only part of the squally mix. Even as they'd banked over the Channel, climbing to fifteen hundred feet, a major winter storm front out of Eastern Europe had forced the planes to fly into a powerful, battering headwind that would rock them throughout the crossing.

Opportunely, the cloud cover broke over France to reveal a striking azure sky. Peering outside, Feigion realized he could see for a hundred miles in any direction—and see the other Skytrains emerge from the front in perfect serial formation. Though it was quite a feat, it didn't surprise him. That day the pilots had taken to the air with a special, steely determination, as if all their training and discipline were being driven by a force beyond their comprehension.

The armada flew straight as a ram over Belgium, its planes steadily trimming altitude until they were at their drop height above the treetops. The crews would remember a featureless plain of snow spreading out around the shadows of their wings, its whiteness blinding them with glare in the unexpected sunlight. As their eyes adjusted, they saw tall pines thrusting upward through the cover, and roads packed with a solid, bumper-to-bumper line of German tanks and other vehicles. Then a chain of low hills running north to south, and finally Bastogne itself in the distance. Surrounded by circular belts of enemy artillery and antiaircraft guns, it resembled the center of a gigantic target.

The Pathfinder signals would guide the planes to their bull's-eye from about twenty miles in. Flying without armaments, the C-47s relied on speed and surprise to accomplish their mission. As one airman recalled, there had been "no fancy tactical planning, no elaborate flight paths" for the armada. The crews were told to head "straight on in, jettison your loads on the position markers west of Bastogne, and get the hell out."

The row of hills across the flight path proved an asset, hiding the planes from the German flak batteries until they were almost at the drop zone. But the guns awoke with a roar as they overflew them on their final approach.

In the cargo holds, the men quickly shoved their freight out the doors under heavy fire. The bundles fell in a growing swarm, a dozen, fifty, a hundred, and then countless hundreds, their color-coded parachutes snapping open above them—yellow chutes for equipment bundles, red for ammunition, white for medical supplies, blue for rations.

Sergeant Ben Obermark, a crew chief aboard one of the flights, found himself staring down in disbelief at the thought of thousands of American soldiers trapped in all that snow, the whiteness spreading out beneath him to the very limits of his vision. Standing in the door, the glare in his eyes, he couldn't see the men or much of anything else down there. On impulse, he knelt on the floor, and then got down lower, lower, until he was lying flat in the aisle, belly to belly with the plane despite the hail of deadly fire pouring up from the enemy emplacements. And then, squinting, shielding his eyes with one hand, flattened and vulnerable inside the door, he was finally able to make out American soldiers. They were on the move, scrambling for the para-bundles dotting the snow-covered ground, and hurriedly dragging them off out of sight.

As his plane veered away from the DZ, its load emptied, the chattering guns behind him, Bastogne behind him, Sergeant Obermark finally stood up and moved from the door. He thought of the guys down there all during the three-hour return trip to England—those cold, desperate men running out for the bundles—and kept hoping the supplies they'd received would give them a chance to hang on awhile longer.

In fact, the supplies enabled them to hang on just long enough.

5.

Yellow, red, white, blue.

At the brick pile, McNiece and the men were watching the supply bundles fall through the suddenly, startlingly, gloriously blue sky like manna on parachutes. The arrival of the planes had also turned the Germans' attention skyward, and led to a welcome pause in the machine-gun fire they'd been directing at the hill.

Yellow, red, white, blue.

Down below the hill and across the road toward the edge of the cemetery, the trucks and jeeps had sped to the DZ as soon as the radars were triggered, arriving to wait for the planes, their crews pouring from the vehicles at first sight of the bundles. Now they were recovering the packages as they touched down on the ground, in some instances gathering supplies from bundles that had come apart in midair or broken to pieces upon landing, the men picking their spilled contents out of the snow and hauling them into the vehicles by the armful. With each new planeload there would be a fresh outburst of cheers from all around the area, the troopers whooping it up like they were at a ballpark in New York, Cleveland, or St. Louis when their team won the World Series.

Yellow, red, white, blue.

Up atop the bricks, Private Jack Agnew kept working the radar, pressing its button once every thirty seconds as he'd learned to do in England. He would rarely climb down off that pile in the next five days, at least not while the sun was out and the planes were coming in. That first day, in the first four hours of the airlift, the Pathfinders guided in 244 planes. The following day—the day before Christmas—they brought in almost 200 more, switching between their three radar locations to keep the Germans from getting a bead on them. On Christmas Day, the weather conditions over England prevented the fleet of C-47s from taking off, but McNiece and his men would bring in a volunteer eleven-glider lift of medical personnel launched from France. There would be 269 transports the day after that, and another hundred plus on the fifth and final day of the drop.

They were long, hard days for Agnew. He was hungry, and thirsty, and most of all he was cold. On one of those days, a foxhole at the bottom of the hill took a direct hit from an artillery shell, and the eight soldiers in it, who'd been talking to him on and off to while away the hours, were blown to death. On Christmas, he and the other Pathfinders got a treat, the troops sharing some hot C rations from the resupply drops—cow beets and onions that were like a taste of heaven after the cold Ks they'd been eating, and that might have warmed the Pathfinders up all the more because of the gratitude they represented. But with the way he was burning calories in the cold, Agnew's hunger and thirst would soon return.

There would be another day when Agnew, briefly relieved from his post, found a pig that had been run over by a tank in the snow. But when he stood the carcass up against a tree, hoping to slice some meat from it, it was stiff as a board, and he dejectedly returned to the brick pile with his growling stomach and wilted dreams of a roasted ham dinner for himself and the boys.

Throughout those days, Agnew would continue to see the burial details hacking bodies out of the snow with the edges of their shovels, the breath steaming from their mouths as they struggled to maneuver their rigid bodies onto the stretchers.

Those days. Long, hard, and always the maddening, bone-deep cold.

Like the rest of the men in Bastogne, Agnew had heard that General George Patton's Third Army was making a breakthrough, and that the German siege was already starting to crumble at its outer edges, and he guessed that was one of the things that got him through.

But the thing that really did it for him, McNiece, and the rest of the men who had jumped to bring in the planes, was just seeing the cargo parachutes descend from the sky with the incoming waves of planes. Up on the bricks as the transports came in, half-frozen, his finger an icicle jabbing at the radar button every thirty seconds, Agnew would watch the chutes spring open above the bundles, yellow, red, white, and blue, and feel his heart lift in his chest.

"It's a great Christmas present," he said to McNiece on the first day. "One these men won't forget for a long time."

He'd been up on the pile with the CRN-4, Jake and the others standing beneath him, all of them using the bricks for cover and watching the parachutes float above them, bright as balloons at a summer fair, or possibly a grand and special birthday celebration.

McNiece watched the bundles thump onto the snow, their chutes flapping in the wind as the soldiers hurried over to bring them back to their trucks.

Delivered by air, he thought.

6.

Lieutenant Everett G. Andrews of the 101st Airborne's 377th Field Artillery Battalion was a Normandy replacement who couldn't have suspected what he'd be in for when he got shipped into Bastogne.

On December 18 his unit had been ordered to set up gun positions on the outskirts of Savy, a farming hamlet near a major road and rail juncture north of the city. Their command post was a small house occupied by the LeRoy family—a farmer, his wife, and their four daughters—and Andrews had known it would be a stress on them when he and three other officers moved in. But they'd done their best to assist the LeRoys with their chores, and had hooked up a small generator to restore the electricity that had been knocked out by German shellings. That gave them lights, and a radio, so they could listen to the BBC. These were good accommodations compared to the cold foxholes the infantrymen had to endure, and Andrews had considered himself most fortunate to be inside.

A day or so after reaching the little village, the officers had sent some trucks out for supplies and ammunition, but they'd never seen them again. Ironically, it was through the BBC news broad-casts that they found out they were surrounded by enemy forces.

Early on the 23rd, Andrews received word from Headquarters about the airborne resupply and was told to be ready for when the flights came through. On a signal from a group of Pathfinders who'd marked out the drop zone, he and his men were to speed out in every available vehicle to assist with collecting the bundles.

Andrews would remain there for all the airdrops, watching the C-47s fly in over a German flak belt situated just beyond the DZ, making them easy targets. He saw transports arrive damaged, some trailing smoke, their engines on fire. But the pilots had kept them in formation long enough to drop their supply loads before the crews bailed . . . though some were unable to escape their air-crafts before they crashed or exploded. It was the bravest act his eyes ever witnessed.

On the ground, there was a danger of getting hit by some of the hundred-fifty and two-hundred-pound bundles that broke free of their chutes in the air, and Andrews took to ducking under the trucks until after a plane dropped its load, only then crawling out to gather the supplies.

Over the course of those days, the troopers assigned to pick up the bundles started hanging on to the parachutes. They'd found all kind of uses for them—they made great outer linings for their boots and bedrolls, and even spare blankets. Andrews took four of them, one of each color, yellow, red, white, and blue.

When Patton thrust through the German defenses the day after Christmas, far ahead of most predictions, Andrews was redeployed to Longchamps, northwest of Bastogne, where elements of the II SS Panzer Corps were staging one of the final enemy attempts to retake the hub. He would remain there until January, when he sustained wounds that sent him back to the States for hospitalization.

But before that he returned to the farmhouse in Savy and gave the light blue parachute to the LeRoy family, explaining that it was a token of appreciation for the courtesy they had shown him and his fellow officers. On his second visit there a year later, Mrs. LeRoy would proudly display the blue dresses she'd sewn out of the fabric for their four daughters.

Andrews left Europe with the yellow, red, and white parachutes in his possession. The white one became his wife Margaret's wedding dress. After the war, in the 1950s, he decided to donate the yellow one to the 101st Airborne Division museum, but still kept the red one as a cherished reminder of the day those planes came in and saved the men in Bastogne.

In 2014, the ninety-three-year-old Andrews learned about a World War Two reenactment group that was planning to stage a para-bundle drop over Bastogne on the seventieth anniversary of the wartime events that occurred there. It was then that he decided the fourth parachute should be used in the commemoration, and got in touch with the group, who accepted it with deep appreciation. The rigging was all fouled up, and Andrews couldn't remember how to fix it, so he gave it to some riggers at Fort Bragg, home of the 82nd Airborne, and they repaired it for him.

"This may be the last one that's fit to use," he would say. "The last of all that fell that day."

Donating it to the group, Everett Andrews decided that he would travel to Belgium with the parachute, return there so he could look up one last time to see it blossom open beneath the wings of a soaring plane in the high, cold winter air of the Ardennes Mountains.

And maybe, he thought, that was why he'd held on to it for so long. So they could go back to Bastogne, both of them, back to where heroes fought and died for something immeasurably greater than themselves, back to where thousands of besieged, weary, desperate American soldiers received the most precious thing of all as a Christmas gift.

Everett Andrews was going back to Bastogne, one last time, to look up and see that dash of red against the blue sky and white clouds, coming gently down to earth, as bright and enduring as hope itself.

7.

The breakthrough of General Patton's 4th Armored Division on December 26, 1944, did not immediately end the fighting in the Ardennes. Although Hitler ordered a retreat in early January, scattered armored elements held out in the Bois Jacques pine woods around the villages of Foy, Noville, and Recogne, north of Bastogne—some because they did not have enough fuel left to return to their side of the line. Ragged but able, the 101st Airborne Division would clear those areas, but only after some of the bloodiest combat of the war.

Snuffy Smith, the original Pathfinder/medic who had dropped on Normandy and Holland, had taken retraining at Chalgrove with the IX TCC in December, but wasn't among the men Jake

McNiece chose for his team or Rothwell's backup stick. Reassigned to the 502nd PIR, he was sent to Bastogne to join Lieutenant John F. Stopka's 3rd Battalion with other reinforcements after Patton's tanks and infantry reopened the roads in late December. As the fighting raged on, the Pathfinders were often used as recons and given the dangerous job of scouting the snowy mountain terrain ahead of the main troops.

In mid-January, Stopka's unit was advancing through the Bois Jacques between Foy and Bizory, moving along one side of a railroad track that had been built up almost twenty feet above the clearing, when they spotted German tanks sheltering on the other side of the berm. The Germans had set up gun emplacements that would have made a ground attack on the tanks all but impossible, and one of Stopka's men radioed for airpower to knock them out.

The fighter planes arrived quickly, strafing and bombing the enemy armor. But their attack came too close to Stopka and his men, leaving thirty dead and forty wounded.

Smith, who would treat the wounded and tag the dead, recalled the attack as the most horrifying experience he had "from D-Day all through the 101st battles," thinking it even worse than watching the glider tows go down over the fields of Holland as he guarded the T with the rest of the Pathfinders. Separating the loose ends of war from its main threads was an exercise for the generals and historians. For the men fighting and dying on the ground, the pattern and perspective remained those of daily survival.

But the fighting in the Ardennes soon would be over. By the end of the month, the last of the German units in Belgium either had been destroyed or were limping back across the lines. Hitler's thrust to divide the U.S.-British alliance and win a compromise peace with them had failed, leaving his country still engaged on two fronts, with nearly all its military resources exhausted, and the armies of the East and West racing toward Berlin.

The Third Reich's days of ascendance were long gone, its everlasting night coming on fast.

8.

In early January, Jake McNiece and his two sticks of Pathfinders were transferred out into France, where they stayed for several days before taking off in a flight for Chalgrove. On their return, Captain Frank Brown of the IX TCC would recommend all of them for Silver Stars for their daring jump into Bastogne, citing valor and gallantry in action. But Colonel Robert Sink, executive officer of the 506th—and the commander of McNiece's Regimental HQ demolition-saboteurs—would quash the request, asserting they had done nothing that wasn't within the range of normal action for paratroopers. McNiece, who cared about as much for medals as for promotions in rank, would react with indifference. "It had not been different from anything else I had ever done," he would say about the mission later on.

Ultimately the men were given Bronze Stars for action and inserted entry. Jake didn't turn his down.

Later that same month, Captain Brown asked Sink's permission to keep McNiece and the five troopers he'd brought from headquarters at Chalgrove. He was again overruled by the colonel.

Send them back to me, Sink cabled. *Evidently, I can kill them quicker than you can!*

Brown would reply that he could have all of the men but McNiece, who was "essential to this operation" and needed for the training of new recruits. In the end, Lieutenant Schrable Williams stayed on too.

Meanwhile, the war was entering its final stages. With the victory at Bastogne behind them, the Allies would make their push across the Rhine throughout the early part of 1945 and encounter mostly weak and disorganized resistance. In February, the 4th and 90th Infantry Divisions were tasked with plowing through the Siegfried Line near the town of Prüm. What was left of the *Wehrmacht* mustered a counterattack that boxed in the American troops at the Prüm bridgehead, depleted their supplies and ammunition, and threatened to inflict heavy casualties.

On short rest, McNiece was ordered to train a new group of Pathfinders that would parachute down inside the enemy perimeter and set beacons for an aerial resupply similar to the one that saved the 101st in Belgium. McNiece and Williams pulled the team into shape and led them on their mission, which went off without a hitch.

Two months later, in April, with no further Pathfinder missions anticipated, McNiece was returned to Regimental Headquarters and rejoined the 506th as a demo-sabo when the unit took control of Hitler's abandoned Bavarian chalet, the Eagle's Nest.

On May 7, 1945, General Alfred Jodl, chief of Germany's High Command, signed his nation's complete and unconditional surrender to the Western Allies at Reims, France.

When he spoke about the war decades afterward, McNiece was dismissive of the Pathfinders' role in the Allied triumph, and specifically the jump into Bastogne.

"It wasn't particularly patriotic of us, it was self-preservation," he said, leaving it to others to call them heroes.

BIBLIOGRAPHY

A great many primary and secondary source materials were used in the preparation of this narrative. These include interviews, letters, declassified action reports and other archival documents, newspaper and magazine stories, official military histories, published books, and various Internet sources.

The dialogue in *First to Jump* is taken entirely from primary sources and interviews, and to that end I owe a special debt to the oral histories of George Koskimaki, and the memoirs of Acting Sergeant Jake McNiece (with Richard Killblane).

War is inherently chaotic, and in instances where there may be conflicting recollections of events, I've used logic and judgment to draw an account that is consistent with available facts. Any errors or omissions that may occur in the telling of the tale are my responsibility alone.

A list of major sources follows.

ARCHIVAL U.S. MILITARY DOCUMENTS (UNCLASSIFIED AND DECLASSIFIED)

Operations of the 101st Airborne Division in the Invasion of France, Army Ground Forces Report No. 116, Headquarters, European Theater of Operations, United States Army WD Observers Board, July 15, 1944 by Charles H. Coates, Colonel, Infantry.

Report of D-Day Pathfinder Activities, 101st Airborne Division Pathfinder Group, APO-472 U.S. Army, July 1, 1944 by Frank L. Lillyman, Captain, 502nd Parachute Infantry, Division Pathfinder Officer.

Report of Pathfinder Employment for Operation Neptune, Headquarters 82nd Airborne Division, Advance Command Post, APO-469—In the Field, June 11, 1944 by M.L. McRoberts, Captain, Infantry, 82nd Airborne Division, Pathfinders.

Annex 12 to Ninth Air Force Tactical Air Plan for Operation Neptune, Headquarters IX Troop Carrier Command, APO-133 U.S. Army, May 2, 1944 by Paul L. Williams, Brigadier General, USA, Commanding.

Regimental Unit Study Number 3, 506 Parachute Infantry Regiment in Normandy Drop, Historical Section, European Theater of Operations, 8-3.1 BB 3 by S.L.A. Marshall, Colonel.

Battalion and Small Unit Study Number 9, Cassidy's Battalion, Historical Section, European Theater of Operations, 8-3.1 BA 9 by S.L.A Marshall, Colonel.

Operations of the 101st Airborne Division in the Airborne Invasion of the Netherlands 17 September–27 September 1944 (Rhineland Campaign), Personal Participation—Battalion Executive of an Airborne AA-AT Battalion, Robert R. Kemm, Major, Infantry.

BIBLIOGRAPHY

Report on Operation Market, Air Invasion of Holland by IX Troop Carrier Command by Paul L. Williams, Major General, USA, Commanding.

AGF Report 449—Pathfinder Teams U.S. 101st Airborne, Division Operation "Market," APO-887, December 12, 1944 by Harvey J. Jablonsky, Colonel, Infantry, WD Observers Board.

Report of Airborne Phase Operation "Market," APO 109, October 5, 1944 by Headquarters XVII Corps, Airborne

Escape and Evasion Report 2307, Faith, Charles M. (1st Lt.), MLR Number UD 133, UD 134 by War Department, U.S. Forces, European Theater, Military Intelligence Service (MIS), Escape and Evasion section (MIS-X).

Memorandum: Pillaging and Plundering, Headquarters 101st Airborne Division, Office of the Division Commander, APO-472, October 17, 1944 by Maxwell D. Taylor, Major General, USA, Commanding.

The Operations of a Regimental Pathfinder Unit, 507th Parachute Infantry Regiment (82nd Airborne Division) In Normandy, France 6 June 1944 (Normandy Campaign) by Captain John T. Joseph, Infantry, Advanced Infantry Officers Class Number Two.

Graphic Survey of Radio and Radar Equipment used by the Army Air Forces, July 1, 1945 by United States Army Air Forces Air Technical Service Command, N-12836-D-2.

Training Progress Report 1 Dec 1944–14 January 45, Headquarters IX TCC Pathfinder Group (Prov.), Office of the Corps Pathfinder Officer, APO-135, 14 January 1945 by Frank L. Brown, Captain, Infantry (Parachute) Corps Pathfinder Officer.

Report of Pathfinder Operation "Nuts," Headquarters IX TCC Pathfinder Group (Prov.) Office of the VXIII Corps, Airborne, June 27, 1945 by Frank L. Brown, Infantry (Parachute) Corps Pathfinder Officer.

Packed Parachute Delivery Supplies at AAF 465, APO 133, January 9, 1945, Headquarters 409th Quartermaster Depot Commander, Marvin F. Jacobs, 1st Lieutenant, QMC, Operations Officer.

Report of Resupply of American Troops in Bastogne Area, Headquarters, IX Troop Carrier Pathfinder Group (Prov.), 1944 by Lieutenant Colonel Joel L. Crouch.

267

Siege of Bastogne, Historical Section, European Theater of Operations, Office of the Chief of Military history by S.L.A. Marshall, Colonel.

BOOKS

Crusade in Europe by General Dwight D. Eisenhower (New York: Doubleday & Company, 1948).

The Memoirs of Field Marshall Montgomery by Viscount Montgomery of Alamein (Cleveland: World Publishing Company, 1958).

Soldier: The Memoirs of Matthew B. Ridgeway by Matthew B. Ridgeway as told to Harold H. Martin (New York: Harper & Brothers, 1956).

On to Berlin: Battles of an Airborne Commander, 1943–1946 by General James M. Gavin (New York: Viking, 1978).

Airborne: World War II Paratroopers in Combat Edited by Julie Guard (United Kingdom: Osprey, 2007).

Easy Company Soldier: The Legendary Battles of a Sergeant from World War II's "Band of Brothers" by Sergeant Don Malarky with Bob Welch (New York: St. Martin's Press, 2008).

In the Footsteps of the Band of Brothers: A Return to Easy Company's Battlefields with Sgt. Forrest Guth by Larry Alexander (New York: New American Library, 2007).

Parachute Infantry: An American Paratrooper's Memoir of D-Day and the Fall of the Third Reich by David Kenyon Webster (Louisiana State University Press, 1994).

The Filthy Thirteen: From the Dustbowl to Hitler's Eagle's Nest: The True Story of the 101st Airborne's Most Legendary Squad of Combat Paratroopers by Richard Killblane and Jake McNiece (Philadelphia: Casemate Publishers, 2003).

Fighting With the Filthy Thirteen: The World War II Story of Jack Womer— Ranger and Paratrooper by Jack Womer and Steven DeVito (Philadelphia: Casemate 2012).

Hugh Nibley: A Consecrated Life by Boyd Jay Peterson (Utah: Greg Kofford Books, 2002).

The Longest Day: June 6, 1944 by Cornelius Ryan (New York: Simon & Schuster, 1959).

A Bridge Too Far by Cornelius Ryan (New York: Simon & Schuster, 1974).

If Chaos Reigns: The Near-Disaster and Ultimate Triumph of the Allied Airborne Forces on D-Day, June 6, 1944 by Flint Whitlock (Philadelphia: Casemate, 2011).

Tonight We Die As Men: The Untold Story of Third Battalion 506 Parachute Infantry Regiment from Toccoa to D-Day by Ian Gardner and Roger Day (United Kingdom: Osprey Publishing, 2009).

Voices of D-Day: The Story of the Allied Invasion, Told by Those Who Were There Edited by Ronald J. Drez (Louisiana State University Press, 1996).

War Stories of D-Day: Operation Overlord: June 6, 1944 by Michael Green and James D. Brown (Norwalk: MBI Publishing, 2009).

American GI in Europe in World War Two, Volume 3 by J.E. Kaufmann and H.W. Kaufmann (Pennsylvania: Stackpole Books, 2009).

Deliver Us from Darkness: The Untold Story of the Third Battalion 506 Parachute Infantry Regiment During Market Garden by Ian Gardner (United Kingdom: Osprey Publishing, 2012).

Band of Brothers: E Company, 506th Regiment, 101st Airborne from Normandy to Hitler's Eagle's Nest by Stephen E. Ambrose (New York: Simon & Schuster, 2001).

Pegasus Bridge, June 6, 1944 by Stephen E. Ambrose (New York: Simon & Schuster, 1988).

Citizen Soldiers: The U.S. Army from the Normandy Beaches to the Bulge to the Surrender of Germany, June 7, 1944–May 7, 1945 by Stephen E. Ambrose (New York: Simon & Schuster, 1997).

September Hope: The American Side of a Bridge Too Far by John C. McManus (New York: New American Library, 2012).

Alamo in the Ardennes: The Untold Story of the American Soldiers Who Made the Defense of Bastogne Possible by John C. McManus (New York: John Wiley & Sons, 2007).

D-Day with the Screaming Eagles by George Koskimaki (New York: Presidio Press, 2006).

Hell's Highway: A Chronicle of the 101st Airborne Division in the Holland Campaign, September–November 1944 by George Koskimaki (Philadelphia: Casemate Publishers, 2003).

Hell's Highway: U.S. 101st Airborne and Guards Armored Division by Tim Saunders (Pennsylvania: Casemate, 2001).

The Battered Bastards of Bastogne: The 101st Airborne and the Battle of the Bulge, December 19, 1944–January 17, 1945 by George Koskimaki (New York: Presidio Press, reissue edition, 2007).

101st Airborne: The Screaming Eagles at Normandy by Mark Bando (New York/London: Zenith Press, 2001).

101st Airborne: The Screaming Eagles in World War II by Mark Bando (New York/London: Zenith Press, 2007).

Avenging Eagles: Forbidden Tales of the 101st Airborne Division in World War 2 by Mark Bando (Michigan: Mark Bando Publishing, 2007).

Into the Valley: The Untold Story of USAAF Troop Carrier Command in World War II from North Africa through Europe by Charles Hutchinson Young (Michigan: PrintComm, 1995).

Battle: The Story of the Bulge by John Toland (New York: Random House, 1959).

The Unknown Dead: Civilians in the Battle of the Bulge by Pete Schrijvers (The University Press of Kentucky, 2005).

ARTICLES

"Lillyman, Invasion Pathfinder, Knew He Was to Lead Invasion," Howard Cowan, *The Syracuse Herald-American*, June 8, 1944.

"Paratrooper Capt. Lillyman, Husband Skaneateles Woman, First Soldier to Land in France," Uncredited, *The Skaneateles Press*, June 9, 1944.

"Capt. Lillyman's Cigar Plays Important Part in Jump, He Once Said," Uncredited, *The Skaneateles Press*, June 9, 1944.

"Soldier at Ease: New York Hotel Treats Paratrooper Veteran to Banana Splits, Fancy Five-Room Suite and Bemushroomed Steaks," Uncredited, *LIFE Magazine*, December 3, 1945.

"D-Day Hero Dies," Uncredited, *Lodi News Sentinel,* March 9, 1971.

"D-Day Remembered," Uncredited, *Air Force News Agency,* June 8, 2006.

"Sergeant Recalls Days under General Taylor," Uncredited, *Kentucky New Era,* June 29, 1959.

"Generals Rise at Dawn Says Lorelle Hearst," Lorelle Hearst, *The Milwaukee Sentinel,* June 10, 1944.

"The Pilot Who Led the D-Day Invasion," Tony Reichhardt, *Air & Space Magazine,* June 6, 2014.

"Supplies Are Dropped to U.S. Troops: Surrounded Men Get Aid as Relief Column Is Nearing London," Associated Press, *The Independent-Record,* December 27, 1944.

"Supplies to Troops: Ammunition Parachuted to Americans in Bastogne Area," Associated Press, *Lawrence Journal-World*, December 27, 1944.

"The Story of the 101st Airborne Division," booklet, Staff, *Stars and Stripes Magazine,* 1945.

"Family Seeks Clues to WWII Mystery of Missing Pilot," Doug Clark, *Ellensburg Daily Record*, March 1, 2001.

"Story Behind a Brick of a Hero," Libby Car, *West Seattle Herald*, July, 27, 2009.

"El Pasoans Went to War as Young Paratroopers," John Hall, *El Paso Times,* November 11, 2010.

"Old Paratroopers Relives Leaps of Faith: 12 D-Day Pathfinders Reunite in Nashville for What May Be Last Time," Leon Alligood, *The Tennessean,* May 20, 2006.

"World War II Veteran Everett Andrews Will Return to Bastogne, Along with Parachute Used in War," *Fayetteville Observer,* Chick Jacobs, March 1, 2014.

"'Filthy 13' Squad Rivaled by None in Leaping Party," Tom Hoge, *Stars and Stripes,* June 8, 1944.

"A Christmas Present for Bastogne," Richard Killblane, *World War II Magazine,* September 2003.

"'Filthy Thirteen' Veterans Recount Their Antics during WWII," Leo Shane III, *Stars and Stripes,* November 10, 2008.

"World War II Soldier John (Jack) Agnew, Whose Unit Inspired 'Dirty Dozen,' Dies at 88," Associated Press, *New York Daily News,* April 12, 2010.

"Jake McNiece, Who Led Incorrigible D-Day Unit, Is Dead at 93," William Yardley, *New York Times,* February 13, 2013

Obituary, Joel L. Crouch, *Honolulu Star-Bulletin*, August 23, 1997.

TRANSCRIPTS/RECORDED INTERVIEWS

Acting Sgt. Jake McNiece, 506th PIR, 101st Airborne, Pathfinder (Series of 15 videotaped interviews), The Witness to War Foundation, WitnesstoWar .org.

Acting Sgt. Jake McNiece and Private John J. Agnew, 506th PIR, Pathfinders, 2009 (video), American Veterans Committee.

Private Reed Williams, 502nd PIR, 101st Airborne, Pathfinder (Series of 6 videotaped interviews), The Witness to War Foundation, WitnesstoWar.org.

Sgt. Maynard "Beamy" Beamesderfer, 501st PIR, 101st Airborne, Pathfinder, and Private Angel Romero, 82nd Airborne, May 26, 2012 (radio), Hometownheroes .com, interview conducted by Paul Loeffler.

Lt. Reed Pelfrey, 502nd PIR, 101st Airborne, Pathfinder, 2011 (video), Curahee Military Museum.

Lieutenant Everett G. Andrews, 377th Field Artillery Battalion, 101st Airborne, August 2001 (transcript), APSU Veterans' Oral History Project.

Lieutenant Everett G. Andrews, 377th Field Artillery Battalion, 101st Airborne, December 2013 (video), 101st Airborne Museum.

INTERNET

For information and links to archival 101st Airborne Pathfinder footage on the web: 502-101airborne.pl/sylwetki/frank-lillyman

For a partial list of Pathfinder teams and aircrews on D-Day: americandday.org

For information about the equipment used by the IX TCC Pathfinders: usair borne.be/Pathfinders/us_pathfinders_historique_txt.htm

For information about HMS *Tartar*: hmstartar.co.uk

For information about motion sickness pills used by paratroopers on D-Day and alleged looting during and after Market Garden: battledetective.com

For information about the makeup and disposition of German troops and antiaircraft batteries in the Netherlands: axishistory.com; regionaalarchieftilburg.nl

For information about 101st Airborne's Battle at Best, in the Netherlands: battleatbest.com/battle-at-best-101st-airborne-division.html

For information about the burial of American war casualties in the Netherlands: adoptiegraven-database.nl

For invaluable information about the fate of IX TCC Pathfinder Flight 42-100981, its crew, and its Pathfinders (with a great debt to the investigative work of Chris Van Kerckhoven): forum.armyairforces.com; bloggen.be/warresearcher; 69th-infantry-division.com/pdf/USArmy69InfDiv_Vol56_No1_Sep Dec2002.pdf.

For information about the 326th Airborne Medical Company: med-dept.com/unit-histories/326th-airborne-medical-company